Learning English, Advanced Modern Practice

Herausgegeben von
Professor Dr. Gerhard Fisch, Fachleiter am Seminar für Studienreferendare, Freiburg i. Br.;
Oberstudienrat Hans Künzig, Lehrbeauftragter am Seminar für Studienreferendare, Freiburg i. Br.;

sowie
Gymnasialprofessor Johannes Greiner, Freiburg i. Br.;
Gymnasialprofessor Helmut Heinemann, Freiburg i. Br.;
Universitätslektorin Eileen Stewart, M.A., Freiburg i. Br.;

unter Mitarbeit von
Akademischer Direktor Dr. Friedrich Ungerer, Universität München

1. Auflage 1 4 3 2 1 /1980 79 78 77

Alle Drucke dieser Auflage können im Unterricht nebeneinander benutzt werden. Die letzte Zahl bezeichnet das Jahr dieses Druckes.

Umschlaggestaltung: Hans Lämmle, Stuttgart.
Druck: Hieronymus Mühlberger KG, Augsburg. Printed in Germany.
ISBN 3-12-506200-4

Learning English

Advanced Modern Practice

Grammatisches Übungsbuch für die Sekundarstufe II

Herausgegeben von G. Fisch und H. Künzig
sowie H. Heinemann, E. Stewart und J. Greiner
unter Mitarbeit von F. Ungerer

Ernst Klett Stuttgart

Vorwort

Advanced Modern Practice ist ein sprachpraktisches Übungsbuch, das die mündliche und schriftliche Ausdrucksfähigkeit des Lernenden fördern und gleichzeitig seine Kenntnis der Formen und Strukturen des Englischen vertiefen will. Es baut auf den in vier bis sechs Jahren Englischunterricht erworbenen Fertigkeiten und Einsichten auf und sucht diese zu festigen und zu erweitern. Damit ist *Advanced Modern Practice* in erster Linie ein Übungsbuch für die Sekundarstufe II, kann aber bereits gegen Ende der Sekundarstufe I eingesetzt werden.

Die einzelnen Kapitel und Teilkapitel müssen nicht in der vorgegebenen Reihenfolge behandelt werden, vielmehr können einzelne Stoffgebiete je nach dem Bedarf der Lerngruppe gezielt ausgewählt werden. Übungen mit erhöhter Leistungsanforderung sind durch ▼ gekennzeichnet.

Die Stoffauswahl wurde von didaktischen Gesichtspunkten bestimmt: ausschlaggebend waren häufige Fehlerquellen, die durch Untersuchungen von Schülerarbeiten und zusätzliche Umfragen festgestellt wurden. Den breitesten Raum im Übungsangebot nehmen die Strukturen aus dem Bereich des Verbums ein, die für deutsche Schüler erfahrungsgemäß eine Hauptfehlerquelle darstellen.

Die Auswahl der Stoffe zielt keineswegs auf Vollständigkeit. Auf solche grammatische Gegenstände wurde verzichtet, die der Schüler nach mehrjährigem Englischunterricht beherrschen sollte, wie z. B. die Formenbildung bei den Zeiten, beim Passiv, beim Adverb usw. (entsprechendes Material findet sich z. T. in dem separat angebotenenen Tonbandprogramm, s. u.). Aufgenommen wurden allerdings solche Stoffgebiete, die selbst Schülern der Sekundarstufe II immer wieder Schwierigkeiten bereiten, auch wenn ein gesicherter Gebrauch bereits auf der Sekundarstufe I erwartet wird. Dies gilt z. B. für die Steigerung des Adjektivs und des Adverbs, für die Stellung der Objekte, für die Wahl der indefiniten Pronomen usw.

Die einzelnen Kapitel enthalten im wesentlichen folgende Elemente:

1. *Refresher Patterns:* Sie stellen eine didaktische Verdichtung umfangreicher Grammatikkapitel dar, wobei grammatische Erläuterungen und Regeln auf Englisch gegeben werden. Sie ermöglichen eine rasche Orientierung sowie die Kontrolle und Rückversicherung bei der Bearbeitung der nachfolgenden Übungen. Durch ihre Einbettung in einen situativen Rahmen bieten sich die Beispielsätze als Merkmuster an.
2. *Belegtexte:* Sie dienen der Veranschaulichung und Analyse sprachlicher Formen und Verwendungsweisen. Zu ihnen gehören auch die *Cartoons*, die für die grammatischen Gegenstände jedes Kapitels idiomatische Belege und zusätz-

liche Sprechanlässe liefern. In den meisten Fällen schließen die Belegtexte weiterführende sprachpraktische Übungen mit ein.

3. *Übungstexte:* Die verschiedenen Übungstypen wie Einsetz-, Austausch-, Umwandlungsübungen, Guided Composition, Übungen zum Text- und Strukturverständnis usw. ermöglichen unterschiedliche Arbeitsformen (schriftlich, mündlich, arbeitsteilige Verfahren, Hausaufgaben etc.). Alle Übungen haben einen situativen Rahmen; die Themen hierzu sind durchweg den Erfahrungsbereichen der Jugendlichen entnommen und bieten damit auch Anregungen für eine Auseinandersetzung mit dem Textinhalt.
4. *Bildgeschichten:* Bei einer weitgehenden Reduzierung sprachlicher Vorgaben dient die Beschreibung und Interpretation von Bildgeschichten der Schulung des eigenständigen Formulierens bzw. der ganzheitlichen Darstellung von Vorgängen und Sachverhalten. Die Umsetzung der bildlichen Darstellungen in sprachliche Aussagen soll den Schüler zu selbständigen Formulierungen führen und damit den Transfer fördern.
5. *Übersetzungen:* Sie sind immer dann ein Teil des Übungsangebots, wenn eine kontrastive Behandlung des Stoffes für den deutschen Schüler nützlich ist.
6. *Literarische Texte:* In zahlreichen Bundesländern sehen die Prüfungsbestimmungen für den Abschluß der Sekundarstufe II unter anderem Aufgaben im Bereich der Form- und Stilanalyse vor. Eine Reihe von Übungen zu den literarischen Texten sollen das bewußte Wahrnehmen besonderer Sprachformen fördern, formale (stilistische) Gestaltungselemente erschließen und damit Grundlagen für die weiterführende Textarbeit schaffen.

Auch auf der Sekundarstufe II sind drillmäßige Übungen notwendig, um den Gebrauch bestimmter Formen und Strukturen systematisch zu festigen. Ergänzend zu *Advanced Modern Practice* wird deshalb ein Tonbandprogramm mit situativ angelegten Übungen angeboten, die sowohl im Sprachlabor als auch im Kontaktunterricht verwendbar sind: *Advanced Structural Practice* (Tonbänder Klett-Nr. 99265; Textbuch Klett-Nr. 99264).

Table of Contents

Tenses and Aspects

Zeichenerklärung

▼ = Übung mit erhöhter Leistungsanforderung

RP Refresher Patterns

Tenses and Aspects

A Present Tense – Simple and Continuous

1 Refresher Patterns

A reporter for a women's magazine is interviewing Mrs Sherwin, the wife of an American composer:

1. Present Tense Simple

Reporter: Mrs Sherwin, your husband **composes** all kinds of music. Can you describe how he normally goes about it?	Chiefly used a) for the statement of facts which are generally known
Mrs Sherwin: First he **plays** the music on the piano and **records** it, then he **plays** the tape over and **writes** the music down.	b) for successive actions
Reporter: I **know** that you come to New York quite often. Does Mr Sherwin ever write music while he is here?	c) with certain verbs when they express a state rather than an activity (cf. list below)
Mrs Sherwin: No, he doesn't. He usually **retires** to our country house.	d) for habitual activities

2. Present Tense Continuous

	Chiefly used for activities of limited duration
Reporter: I believe your husband **is working** on another musical?	a) in progress, but not necessarily at the moment of speaking
Mrs Sherwin: As a matter of fact, he **is going** over the manuscript at this moment.	b) in progress at the moment of speaking
Reporter: I'm afraid, it**'s getting** late. Thank you, Mrs Sherwin.	c) expressing gradual development

The most common verbs that are normally used in the simple form only:

realize	consist of	notice	prefer	seem
recognize	contain	see	like	appear
know	belong to	hear	hate	
believe	possess			

But frequently used in the continuous form: stand, sit, lie, wait, wear.

2 A Hard Day's Night

1. *Describe what the people in the pictures are doing.*
2. *Describe what the manager and the gardener do every day.*

3 Music Inspires

Put in the simple or continuous form of the present tense.

Father: For goodness sake, what (Bob – do) upstairs?

Mother: I (believe) he (do) his homework.

Father: How can he be doing his homework if the radio (blare) like mad?

Mother: You (know) he always (listen) to music when he (do) his homework.

Father: No one can possibly concentrate while all that noise (go on).

Mother: It's just that he (like) music. He says music (inspire) him.

Father: A noise like that (wipe) the last sensible idea out of a person's mind, that's what it (do).

Mother: I've just read an article which (say) that today most young people (listen) to music while they (study).

Father: Any noise, if it's loud enough, (ruin) a person's health. That's a known fact. The only people in the world who (not realize) this (seem) to be you and your son Bob.

Mother: Oh come on, Dad, it (get) more and more difficult to please you, and it always (end up) the same way: You (come) home, (slump) into that chair, and (demand) a cup of tea and the paper. After that, you (try) to find a reason to get mad at Bob, and finally you (blame) me for what you (think) is wrong with him.

Father: It's just that I (think) that every hard-working man (have got) a right to find some peace and quiet when he (come) home. Bob! Bob!! What the hell (he – do) now? Look at that lamp up there! It (shake)!

Mother: He (do) the "Honka-Donka". That's what all the young people (dance) these days.

Praying for Rain?

Deep in the jungle a missionary comes across a witch doctor who is pounding furiously on a drum. The missionary is fascinated by the scene and asks in pidgin English, "What is witch doctor beating drum for?" "We have no water," is the native's reply. "So you're praying for rain?" asks the missionary. "Don't be so stupid," snarls the witch doctor. "I'm sending for the plumber."

4 All's Well That Begins Well

The following text describes the difficulties of an American couple, Buckley and Peg, in getting accustomed to English habits. They have bought a house in England and are now waiting for workmen to come and do some repair work.

Put in the simple or continuous form of the present tense.

At first you (think) you are lucky not to be living in the house while all the repair work (go on). However, you may be startled to discover that for the first few months nothing (go on). You (drive) up to the house every day and (look in). No one is there. Nothing has changed, except that the garden (get) wilder and wilder.

But one day you (notice) action: "Oh, Buckley, look! There's a truck in the drive!"

"Good! It (start). They (really – do) something, too! (You – hear) that roaring noise? It (sound) like blowtorches!"

You are eager to welcome the workmen, excited to find out what they (do) first: "Not here, Peg. It (sound) like it (come) from the laundry."

The sound (grow) louder and louder. Rushing into the laundry you (see) a group of men gathered tensely around a structure of bricks, on the tile floor. One (hold) a blowtorch, and another (steady) a kettle.

"Why, Buckley, they (make) *tea*!"

Adapted from *How To Live Like A Lord Without Really Trying*, by Shepherd Mead, Macdonald & Co., London 1964

Annotations

to be startled to be surprised or alarmed – **the drive** the way leading up to the house – **blowtorch** apparatus for directing a very hot flame on s.th. – **to gather tensely** to stand together and wait in anxiety or excitement – **tile floor** Fliesenbelag – **to steady** to hold s.th. so that it does not move

5 The Eye-catcher

men: sit; read

firemen: rush by; pull a fire-hose along
men: not see; not realize

horse: shoot past; whirl up
lady: throw up her arms; cry
men: not notice; seem unmoved

bankrobber: run away from; wear
policeman: try to catch; fire
men: not hear; read

lion: chase; look blood-thirsty
people: try to escape; run for their lives
men: not look at; hold

girl: walk by; wear; have
men: not read any longer; stare at; like

1. *Describe what is going on in each picture. Do not connect into a plot.*
2. *Describe what happens while the men are sitting on the bench in the park. Give one sentence for each picture. This time connect your sentences into a plot.*

6 Venice

1. *Put in the simple or continuous form of the present tense.*

Venice (lie) in the Lagoon of Venice, about two and a half miles from the mainland. It (extend) over some 120 islands. Few cities (contain) as many artistic treasures and historical monuments. That is why it (attract) so many tourists every summer. They (admire) its wonderful architecture, magnificent frescoes and splendid sculptures.

Many of these tourists, however, (not know) that it may be impossible to enjoy these pleasures in a generation or two. As a result of ice melting at the Poles, the sea level (gradually – rise) from year to year. So the islands (steadily – sink). Nowadays flooding (occur) frequently. Air pollution (also – cause) a lot of damage to the city's art treasures. Ferryboat exhausts and factory chimneys (give off) fumes. Since many houses along the canals (fall) to pieces, the inhabitants (leave) them by the hundreds.

Steps (now – be taken) to save endangered art treasures. Specialists (restore) paintings and statues. International organizations, like UNESCO, (support) the magistrate and the Government in their struggle for the preservation of Venice.

2. *Answer the following questions. Use a different verb in each sentence.*
   a) *What creates the unique charm of Venice, geographically and culturally?*
   b) *What are the dangers threatening it?*
   c) *What is being done to save Venice and its works of art?*

7 Summarizing Texts

▼ For the following exercises keep in mind that summaries are generally introduced by the *present continuous*. However, as soon as there is a transition to successive actions the *present simple* predominates (cf. RP, p. 9, 1b).

Summarize the main points of these texts:
1. *The Ballad of Grand Canyon, p. 149*
2. *A Fine Christmas, p. 24*
3. *Shooting an Elephant, p. 106*
4. *Disarmament, p. 70*

8 Who Said Life Was Easy?

Study the following passage from Erica Jong's novel "Fear of Flying" where she describes a moment of deep personal crisis in the life of her heroine, a young poet:

What was so terrible about being alone? Try to think of the reason, I told myself. Try.

Me: Why is being alone so terrible?

Me: Because if no man loves me I have no identity.

Me: But obviously that isn't true. You write, people read your work and it matters to them. You teach and your students need you and care about you. You have friends who love you.

Me: None of that makes a dent in my loneliness. I have no man. I have no child.

Me: You want freedom and you also want closeness and very few people ever find that.

Me: I know.

Me: Why do you expect to be happy when most people aren't?

Me: I feed on this expectation. It keeps me alive.

Me: Who said life was easy?

Me: No one.

Me: Then why are you so afraid of being alone?

Me: We're going round in circles.

Me: That's one of the troubles with being alone.

Hopeless. I cannot reason myself out of this panic. My breath is coming in short gasps and I am sweating profusely. Try to describe the panic, I tell myself. Pretend you're writing. Put yourself in the third person. But it's impossible. I am sinking into the center of the panic. It seems I am being torn asunder by wild horses and that my arms and legs are flying off in different directions.

From *Fear of Flying*, by Erica Jong, Martin Secker & Warburg Ltd, London.

Annotations

none of that makes a dent in none of that has any effect on – **to feed on** *here:* to be entirely dependent on – **profusely** very much

1. *In one part of the text the author makes use of the simple present tense only, while in another part she prefers the continuous form. Explain the use of these different forms of aspect.*
2. *Write a summary of the contents of this passage:* A young woman is going through a deep personal crisis. She asks …

B Present Perfect – Simple and Continuous

9 Refresher Patterns

1. Present Perfect Continuous

Mary **has been taking** driving lessons for six weeks.	Activity begun in the past, extending up to or into the present The emphasis is on the continuity of the activity
She **has been learning** to drive since early October.	Especially with verbs like: wait, sit, rest, sleep, lie, learn, try, live

2. Present Perfect Simple

David **has passed** his driving test. Now he is allowed to drive a car.	a) Past activity; its result is evident in the present The emphasis is on the result of the activity
Alan **has failed** his driving test at least five times.	b) Repeated activity (often with numbers) in the past; its result is evident in the present

Note: For verbs which are usually not used in the continuous form, cf. RP, p. 9

1.
"Not only have I been drinking, Alice, but I have won Bert Higg's wife at poker."

2.
"You've done the crossword again!"

10 Snow White – A Radio Commercial

Interviewer: You work in the meat department of a supermarket, Mrs Smudge, don't you?

Mrs Smudge: Yes, sir, I've been working here for over seven years now.

Interviewer: Seven years! Let me see – that's roughly 2,100 days behind that counter, and on every single one of those days you've been trying to look spick and span.

Mrs Smudge: Oh well, it has been a problem, most of the time. And I've tried out all sorts of detergents to get my overall clean.

Interviewer: But you've never been wholly satisfied, have you?

Mrs Smudge: I'm afraid not. In a way I've given up hope.

Interviewer: Mrs Smudge, have you ever tried *Snow White?*

Mrs Smudge: I've been told about it – but aren't they all the same? I doubt if ... (Sound fades)

Interviewer: For seven years Mrs Smudge has been slaving over her laundry trying to get rid of those ugly spots and stains which are inevitable with the kind of work she does. We've given her one of *Snow White's* King Size Super Drums. Let's see what she thinks of it:

Hello, Mrs Sm ... should I say Mrs Snow White?! You're certainly looking radiant this morning! Now, will you tell our listeners whether you've changed your mind about detergents in the meantime?

Mrs Smudge: I certainly have! I've been using *Snow White* for six weeks now. I've done all my laundry with it, even my overall, and it certainly has changed my mind! I've just bought another *Snow White* King Size Super Drum and I'll never ... (Sound fades)

Interviewer: You've heard it yourselves, ladies – it's *Snow White* that changes people's minds!

Have you ever given it a thought?

Have you ever wondered how to solve *your* wash-day problems?

Have you ever wanted to make *your* laundry white – whiter – *Snow White?*

Snow White is the answer!

Annotations

commercial advertisement on radio or TV – **spick and span** bright, clean and tidy – **detergent** washing powder or liquid – **to fade** to go slowly out of hearing – **radiant** (of a person, his looks, eyes) bright, showing joy

1. *Explain the use of the present perfect continuous in the text.*
2. *Use the present perfect simple or continuous*
   a) *to say what Mrs Smudge's work and washing problems have been like for the past seven years;*
   b) *to describe her experiences with Snow White.*
3. *Commercials sometimes consist of two parts:*
   a) *the customer describes a problem which he has had for a long time;*
   b) *after he has been given product X or Y, he tells people about the "wonderful" effect it has had.*
   Make up a commercial with the following key words, using the present perfect simple or continuous.
   Customer: Miss Scent, an air hostess
   Product: Seventh Heaven, a deodorant

a) – *the problem*	b) – *the "wonderful" effect*
work	*use*
worry	*get rid of*
never feel confident	*regain confidence*
try out	*feel completely at ease since*
not find a solution	*go out with*
be told	*enjoy*
decide	*buy*
	recommend

11 John and Mary

John and Mary have been married for five years. Make sentences with the following phrases. Use the present perfect simple or continuous:

1. Since you got up ... sit around doing nothing
2. read comics all day long, as usual
3. not stop reading "Superman" since you left school
4. not start to grow up yet
5. The baby ... cry non-stop for an hour, and you ... not lift a finger to help me
6. never once give the baby the feeding-bottle
7. The water-pipe ... leak for three weeks, and you ... not repair it yet
8. come home late the last five nights
9. Your hair ... not see a comb for weeks
10. get on my nerves all morning
11. I ... wait for ages for you to show some sign of life
12. not listen to a word I've said

12 Parliamentary Rhetoric

Put in the simple or continuous form of the present perfect.

Mr Speaker, I thank you for the opportunity to address this House. I (wait) impatiently for the last twenty minutes to catch your eye. During this time I (listen) to what the Honourable Member for Nottingham (have) to say on this important issue, and I must sadly admit that I (seldom hear) a more confused or less exact version of the truth. I don't know how the Honourable Gentleman (spend) his time at the breakfast table recently, but might I suggest that he might (do) well to read the newspaper? (He – live) in dreamland? (He – not watch) TV at all this week? Surely he must be aware that the headlines for the last four days (contain) practically no other news than the subject of today's debate. We must be grateful to the press, for through it, it (be made clear) to everyone that some members of this House (try) to mislead the people of this country. And this is by no means the first occasion on which the members of the Government (act) in this manner. The question is whether or not the Government (realize) what's going on in this country, or could it be that they (want) to hide the truth from the public? If so, they certainly (succeed). The cost of a licence (remain) the same for over ten years. Now is the time to increase it. Otherwise in a very short time there will be more dogs in this country than human beings.

13 **In the Visitors' Galleries** (Translation)

▼ *For your translation keep in mind that German* Präsens *(especially when used with "schon") and* Imperfekt *may require different tenses in English.*

Volker sitzt schon seit beinahe zwei Stunden auf der Besuchergalerie des Unterhauses, als sein Freund Rainer eintrifft. Sie sind beide Angehörige einer Gruppe deutscher Studenten, die London besuchen.

1. *Rainer:* Sitzt du den ganzen Abend schon hier?
2. *Volker:* Ich bin seit ungefähr neun Uhr hier.
3. *Rainer:* Hat sich irgend etwas Interessantes getan (happen)?
4. *Volker:* Bis jetzt haben fünf oder sechs Sprecher Reden gehalten.
5. *Rainer:* Wer spricht gerade?
6. *Volker:* Ein Parlamentsmitglied von (for) Nottingham. Er spricht jetzt schon zwanzig Minuten.
7. *Rainer:* Sieh mal den Mann dort hinten!
8. *Volker:* Er liegt schon seit einer halben Stunde dort. Und sein Nachbar hat die Füße auf dem Sitz vor sich, seitdem ich vor zwei Stunden hereinkam.
9. *Rainer:* Hast du schon mal so was gesehen!
10. *Volker:* Nein. Warst du schon mal zuvor im Parlament?
11. *Rainer:* Ich hatte noch nie Gelegenheit [dazu], obgleich dies mein zweiter Besuch in London ist. – Gehen wir! Ich glaube nicht, daß es sich heute abend lohnt, die Debatte anzuhören.
12. *Volker:* Ich warte jetzt schon beinahe zwei Stunden, daß der Premierminister spricht, und ich möchte ihn nicht verpassen.

C Past Tense – Simple and Continuous

14 Refresher Patterns

Past Tense Continuous

1. a) "What **were** you **doing** yesterday?"
"I **was washing** the car."

The emphasis is on the continuity of the activity

b) "While I **was washing** it the children **were clearing** out the garage."

The emphasis is on activities in progress at the same time

Past Tense Simple

2. a) "What **did** you **do** yesterday?"
"I **washed** the car."

The emphasis is on the completion of the activity.

b) "I **washed** the car while the children **cleared** out the garage."

The emphasis is on completed activities carried out at the same time

c) "Then I **refilled** the water tank. After that I **checked** the battery and **changed** the tyres."

Successive actions

3. "While I **was changing** the tyres	the telephone **rang.**"
Activity in progress	New activity taking place

Note: For verbs which are not usually used in the continuous form, cf. RP, p. 9.

1.
"And how fast were you going when the examiner jumped out?"

2.
"We did the dishes for you, Mum. Dad washed, Peter wiped, and I picked up the pieces."

15 I Only Wanted to Go to London ...

1. *Put in the simple or continuous form of the past tense.*

I (wait) in the departure lounge of Glasgow Airport for my plane to London when two well-dressed gentlemen (come in). One of them (attract) my attention immediately. He (wear) a blue coat, exactly the same colour as my skirt, and (swing) one of those elegant thin umbrellas in his left hand.

As we (walk out) to the plane it (rain) heavily and he politely (offer) me his umbrella. On the gangway he quickly (turn round) to the other man and I (hear) him mumble something to him.

He (sit down) beside me in the plane and his friend (take a seat) directly behind me. Even then I (not notice) anything suspicious about their behaviour. I (enjoy) the man's conversation and the time (pass) quickly. While he (buy) some tobacco from the air-hostess I (look round) to see what his friend (do).

You can imagine my horror when I (see) that he (point) a revolver at me! "Hijackers!" I (scream) terrified at the top of my voice. The next thing that (happen) was that something (hit) me terrifically hard on the back of the head. I (fall) forward and then everything (go black).

When I (come to oneself) two stern-looking gentlemen (stare) at me. I gradually (realize) that they (sit) at the side of the hospital bed in which I (lie).

The moment I (open) my eyes one of them (begin) to fire questions at me: "(you – know) the two men you talked to on the plane? Why (you – shout) 'Hijackers'? (you – notice) what the man was doing who (sit) behind you? Who (sit) next to him? (he – threaten) you with his revolver?"

I (close) my eyes again wondering what this was all about. The last thing I (hear) was one of the policemen saying: "Verdammt noch mal! Jetzt ist sie wieder weg!"

▼ 2. *Imagine you had been an eye-witness of the incident in the plane. Write your own version of what happened after the narrator was hit on the head.* "I was sitting in the same row as the lady. The air-hostess ... when suddenly ..." *Go on:* utter a scream – hit the lady on the head – jump to their feet – hijacker – announce – "no need to panic – remain in your seats" – to the cockpit – sit there trembling – make the lady comfortable – cover her with a blanket – gangster – reappear – captain – explain – "in the interests of the passengers' safety – alter our course" – land in Frankfurt – carry the lady off the plane – six passengers including myself – allowed to leave the plane – after refuelling – unknown destination

16 A Whodunit

1. Miss Butler has been murdered. Her brother has found her in her room and called the police. He tells them what he knows about the time from shortly before the murder until they arrived on the scene of the crime.
   Connect the following sentences by using "when", "as", "while", "and" or "but". Decide whether to use the past simple or the past continuous.

a) after dinner … work in my study	– my sister … write letters in her room
b) later … read	– hear a scream
c) jump to my feet	– rush out of the room
d) run up the stairs	– hear a shot
e) open the door	– see … lying on the floor
f) blood … flow from	– not move
g) bend down	– realize … not breathe
h) wonder what to do	– hear footsteps
i) open the window	– notice a man running to a car
j) run to the telephone	– call the police

Annotation
whodun(n)it popular name for a detective story or murder mystery; from "who has done it"

2. Inspector MacDonald from Scotland Yard turns up a quarter of an hour later. Constable Smith tells him what Mr Butler has said: "He was working in his study, while his sister was writing letters in her room …"
   Now shut your books and continue his report.

17 A Stormy Party

Connect the following sentences by using "while" or "when"; where this is not possible use "but". Decide whether to use the past simple or the past continuous.

1. Mrs Usher (finish) the preparations for her cold supper	her husband (arrange) the tables and chairs on the lawn
2. a light breeze (blow)	otherwise the weather (appear) promising
3. Tom (light) the lanterns	the first guests (arrive)
4. an hour or so later everybody obviously (enjoy) the party	they (wonder) secretly if there was to be anything to eat

5. the older guests (chat and drink)	most of the younger ones (prefer) to dance
6. Mr Usher (ask) his son's girlfriend Betty for the pleasure of a slow waltz	his wife and son Tom (look at) him in a funny sort of way
7. the slow waltz (be played)	Mrs Usher suddenly (switch off) the tape-recorder and (announce): "Supper is served."
8. the guests (walk out) into the garden	she (give) first Betty and then her husband a very meaningful look
9. the guests (help oneself) to Mrs Usher's delicious cold supper	a terrific clap of thunder (shake) the air and the first drops of rain (begin) to fall
10. everyone (run) back into the house	Mrs Usher (try) to rescue as much as she could
11. they (clear up) after the party	Mrs Usher (say): "How glad I am the 'storm' is over!"
12. Mr Usher (look at) his wife closely	he (seem) to detect a twinkle in her eye

18 A Fine Christmas

It was on the afternoon of the day of Christmas Eve, and I was in Mrs Prothero's garden with her son Jim. It was snowing. It was always snowing at Christmas.

We never heard Mrs Prothero's first cry from her house at the bottom of the garden. But soon the voice grew louder.

"Fire!" cried Mrs Prothero, and she beat the dinner-gong. And we ran down the garden, with snowballs in our arms, toward the house: and smoke, indeed, was pouring out of the dining room, and the gong was bombilating, and Mrs Prothero was announcing ruin like a town crier in Pompeii.

We bounded into the house, laden with snowballs, and stopped at the open door of the smoke-filled room. Something was burning all right; perhaps it was Mr Prothero, who always slept there after midday dinner with a newspaper over his face. But he was standing in the middle of the room, saying, "A fine Christmas!" and smacking at the smoke with a slipper.

"Call the fire brigade," cried Mrs Prothero, as she beat the gong.

"They won't be there," said Mr Prothero, "it's Christmas."

There was no fire to be seen, only clouds of smoke and Mr Prothero standing in the middle of them, waving his slipper as though he were conducting.

"Do something," he said.

And we threw all our snowballs into the smoke – I think we missed Mr Prothero – and ran out of the house to the telephone box.

Abridged from *Quite Early One Morning*, by Dylan Thomas. Dent and Sons Ltd., London 1952. Reprinted by permission of the trustees of the Dylan Thomas literary estate.

Annotations

to bombilate a word invented by Dylan Thomas in imitation of the sound of a gong – **to bound** to jump – **to smack** to strike, hit – **to conduct** to control and lead an orchestra

1. a) *Write down the phrases describing the boys' actions. (State only what they actually did.)*
   b) *Say which form (simple or continuous) the author uses to describe the boys' actions and explain why.*
2. a) *Write down the phrases describing circumstances. (This time do not state the persons' actions.)*
   b) *Say which form (simple or continuous) the author uses to describe circumstances and explain why.*
3. *Write down the story as seen through Mr Prothero's eyes.*
4. *The subject-matter in this text is obviously humorous. This humorous effect is heightened by the author's language and style. Find examples of*
   a) *similes* [ˈsimiliz], *comparison of one thing to another;*
   b) *onomatopoeia* [ˌɔnəmætəˈpiə], *formation of words in imitation of sounds;*
   c) *alliteration;*
   d) *hyperbole* [haiˈpəːbəli], *exaggerated statement;*
   e) *irony.*

D Present Perfect and Past Tense – Compared and Contrasted

19 Refresher Patterns

For two hours Joe has been trying in vain to get in touch with his friend Ben. Finally, at ten o'clock, he discovers Ben working in his garden.

moment of speaking

8.00 – 9.00 – 10.00 1. *Joe:* What **were** you **doing** between 8 and 9 o'clock? 2. I **tried** to call you several times.	**past tense continuous:** to express the continuity of an activity in the past **past tense simple:** to express the completion of an activity in the past
8.00 – 10.00 3. *Ben:* I**'ve been working** here since 8 o'clock. 4. As you see, I**'ve cut** the whole hedge.	**present perfect continuous:** to express the continuity of an activity which was begun in the past and extends into the present **present perfect simple:** to express the result of an activity which was begun in the past; the result is evident in the present

1.
"One thing you've learned, friend, they weren't bluffing."

2.
"No you haven't passed – but the way you swore at pedestrians was delightful!"

20 Big Ben

The familiar chimes of what is probably the world's most famous clock, Big Ben in London, stopped for two days last week. Big Ben has sounded the time day and night for nearly a century and a quarter, and for many Britons the chimes have become part of their daily lives. But they had to do without the chimes for two days last week, while workmen were cleaning and painting the clockroom. Originally called the Great Clock of Westminster, Big Ben has been known under its present name since the lifetime of Sir Benjamin Hall, a rather large and burly gentleman, who was Britain's Commissioner of Works when the clock's bell was cast. Big Ben has held a special place in the hearts of many Britons since the last World War, when the BBC regularly broadcast its famous chimes.

Adapted from *News of the Week*, 28th January 1976

Annotations
chimes sounds of a bell – **burly** big and strong – **Commissioner of Works** Beauftragter für Staatsbauten – **to cast a bell** eine Glocke gießen

Pick out from the text all the phrases (noun + verb) which contain the past or present perfect tense. Say which adverbials of time or time clauses make the use of these tenses necessary; if there is no adverbial, explain the use of the tenses from the context.

21 Strange Things Happen to You

1. *The following is a summarized version of Somerset Maugham's short story "The Verger":*

When the new vicar took over St. Peters, he pretty soon let me know that – although I had done my work quite satisfactorily – he wanted me to learn to read and write or I would have to go. I told him that I thought I was too old a dog to learn new tricks and even if I could learn now, I didn't know if I should want to. And that was the end of my career as a verger of St. Peter's.

When I left the church that day I felt that a cigarette would comfort me, and since I didn't carry any with me I looked about for a tobacconist, but couldn't find any among those numerous shops in the vicinity of St. Peter's. Then an idea struck me: They certainly could do with a tobacconist down here! The following day I found a little shop to let and shortly afterwards set up business as a tobacconist. All this happened ten years ago.

Now complete the following text by using the present perfect or the past tense.

Since then I (do) quite well. It (not take) me long to realize that if I (can) run one shop I (can) run half a dozen. And indeed, I (do) so well since, that in the meantime I (take over) several shops and (put) managers in to run them. Today I might say that this (be) quite a success. For many years, whenever I (walk) about London and whenever I (find) a long street that (have) no tobacconist and a shop to let I (take) it. In the course of these ten years I (acquire) no less than ten shops and it is no secret today that I (make) a great deal of money.

The other day the manager of my bank (want) to see me. He (suggest) that I should invest my money. "Sir," I said, "I (never – want) to take any risk, for as long as I can remember. And I (never – have) anything to do with stocks and shares, nor would I know what to do with them. I shouldn't even know what I was signing," I (tell) him, "because" – and that (make) him jump from his chair – "I can't read." "Do you mean to say that you (build up) this important business without being able to read and write?!" he (burst out). "Well, sir," I (say), "that's just it!" "Oh no!" he (cry), "what might have become of you if you had been able to!" "I can tell you, sir," I said, "I'd be verger of St. Peter's!"

Adapted from *The Verger*, by W. Somerset Maugham.

Annotations

verger Kirchendiener (Küster) – **vicar** Gemeindepfarrer (Church of England) – **vicinity** neighbourhood – **a shop to let** a shop that can be rented – **stocks and shares** capital (money) invested in a company

2. *Some time later the bank manager happened to make the acquaintance of the vicar of St. Peter's and of course brought up the subject of his former verger.*
Fill in the missing parts of the story. Use the present perfect or the past tense.

Bank manager: Tell me, sir, did you ever have a verger by the name of Albert Edward?

Vicar: Why, yes. He … for ten years, but I … because …

Bank manager: Do you know what …?

Vicar: I never …

Bank manager: I can tell you! Since … he …

Vicar: Who … ?

Bank manager: … himself … build up …

Vicar: … read and write in the meantime?

Bank manager: No …

22 Pen-friends

1. *Brian Frost and Hans Bauer have just become pen-friends. Brian wants to know as much as possible about Hans and asks him a lot of questions in his first letter. Answer these questions for Hans in English using the words and phrases given on the right.*

a) Have you had a pen-friend before?	2 pen-friends so far
b) Have you ever been to Britain?	never
c) How often have you spent your holidays abroad?	in 1976 and 1977
d) Have you always attended the same school?	always
e) Have you ever played soccer for your school?	two years ago
f) Have you ever had a holiday job?	last summer
g) Have you ever met any British people?	never
h) Have you ever gone camping?	when I was a Boy Scout
i) Have you started learning to drive yet?	last month
j) Has your father ever let you drive his car?	once ... but never since

2. *When Hans writes to Brian he asks him just as many questions. Translate his questions using either the present perfect or the past tense. For your translation keep in mind that German* Präsens *(especially when used with "schon") and* Imperfekt *may require different tenses in English.*

a) Wie lange wohnt ihr schon in Nottingham?
b) Lernst du schon lange Deutsch?
c) Wann habt ihr eure letzten Prüfungen gehabt?
d) Wie lange besuchst du schon deine jetzige Schule?
e) Hast du das Fußballspiel England – Deutschland im Fernsehen gesehen?
f) Wie oft warst du schon in London?
g) Bist du schon einmal mit dem Flugzeug geflogen?
h) Warst du schon einmal im Ausland?
i) Wo hast du deine letzten Sommerferien verbracht?
j) Bist du schon einmal auf einem Pop-Festival gewesen?

23 Blackout

▼ *Put in suitable verbs in the present perfect or the past tense.*

Experts predict that we may be faced with a serious shortage of energy in the near future. If they are right, we might, one of these days, find ourselves in a situation like the one described below.

1. Last Monday the overloaded generators of our city ... .
2. Since then we ... a complete blackout.
3. No electric cooker! I ... a single cup of coffee or tea for three days.
4. No refrigerator! We ... nothing but bread with soft butter and half-melted cheese.
5. No elevator! I seldom ... up and down so many stairs in my life.
6. No vacuum cleaner! My wife just ... the usefulness of the old-fashioned broom again.
7. No dishwasher! You should have seen the mountain of dishes we ... by hand yesterday. With cold water, of course.
8. No TV! We all ... how often we ... it on before.
9. The first two days we still ... some music and the news on the transistor radio, but on Wednesday the batteries ... .
10. Until last night we still ... candles, so we ... read in the evening, but now they are all gone.
11. But there are some advantages, too. Yesterday my wife ... me to mow the lawn! I just ... the electric mower with a grin.
12. On Monday the children ... practically nothing but ice-cream, because the deep-freezer in our supermarket ..., and free ice-cream ... to everybody.

24 The Race for Energy

1. *Complete the following text using the present perfect or the past tense.*

A gigantic race to exploit nature's energy reserves (go on) ever since, in 1973, the industrialized countries (be hit) by the worst energy crisis in memory. Since that time hectic activity (set in) all over the world in an attempt to open up new sources of energy. Enormous sums (be invested) to erect huge oil drilling platforms on the open sea and on the Arctic ice. Costly experiments, too, (be started) to make use of solar energy. At the same time the efforts to produce nuclear energy (be increased) considerably in most countries.

Late in 1973, during the Yom Kippur War between Israel and her Arab neighbours, the oil exporting countries (cut) all supplies to Western Europe and the United States in order to make them reconsider their support of Israel. This (lead) to drastic measures: petrol (be rationed), speed limits (be introduced), all traffic (come) to a complete standstill at weekends when no private cars (be allowed) on the road. Schools (be closed) for lack of heating, and production in some factories (be stopped).

Today we know that those events (not only – cause) changes in world economics and politics but (also – create) a new awareness of our utter dependence on the world's sources of energy.

Until 1973 most western countries (take) their access to cheap energy sources like coal and oil for granted. They (be encouraged) in an often wasteful use of these resources as they (rely) completely on the continued supply from countries which (seem) in no position to refuse the exploitation of their cheap raw material. Since then many of the developing countries (become aware) of the economic power they possess – and make use of it.

The oil crisis of 1973 (have) some side-effects, too. It (remind) the industrialized countries that their high standard of living (very often – be achieved) by underpaying other nations for their raw material. Furthermore, the crisis (warn) people to stop wasting energy as it (become clear) that the world's natural resources are no longer unlimited.

Annotations

solar energy energy produced by the sun – **Yom Kippur** a Jewish holiday (Bußtag) on which, in 1973, the war began; on October 17th the Arab oil producers announced a cut in oil supplies until Israel withdrew from the occupied territories – **to reconsider** to think over and possibly change one's opinion – **utter** complete – **access** opportunity of reaching and using

2. *Say what you know about*

a) *the way in which the industrialized countries exploited sources of energy before the 1973 oil crisis;*

b) *the causes and immediate consequences of the 1973 oil crisis;*

c) *recent attempts to open up new sources of energy;*

d) *the side-effects of the 1973 oil crisis.*

25 The End of American Optimism (Translation)

▼ *For your translation keep in mind that German* Präsens *(especially when used with "schon") and* Imperfekt *may require different tenses in English.*

1. Als ich nach 15 Jahren letztes Jahr in die Vereinigten Staaten zurückkehrte, bemerkte ich einen tiefen Wandel in der Einstellung der meisten Amerikaner.
2. Einer meiner amerikanischen Freunde bestätigte meine Beobachtung: in jüngster Zeit (in recent years) verbreiten sich Unbehagen (uneasiness) und Pessimismus.
3. „Schon seit einer ganzen Weile stimmt etwas nicht (go wrong) in den Vereinigten Staaten", sagte er.
4. „Was ist geschehen?" fragte ich ihn und erinnerte ihn an den amerikanischen Fortschrittsglauben.
5. Hier ist seine Antwort: „Mehr als 200 Jahre lang war die ständige Verbesserung des Lebensstandards ein Glaubensgrundsatz (article of faith) in den Vereinigten Staaten.
6. Aber in den frühen sechziger Jahren begann das Realeinkommen der meisten Amerikaner zu stagnieren.
7. Seit dieser Zeit weicht (give way to) der traditionelle amerikanische Optimismus der Skepsis.
8. Einige der Ursachen wurden während der politischen und sozialen Wirren der späten sechziger und frühen siebziger Jahre deutlich.
9. Das Problem ist jedoch nicht neu. Es besteht schon seit langem. Während der beiden Jahrhunderte unserer Geschichte als Nation sind ungeheure Reichtümer angehäuft (amass) worden.
10. Erst in den letzten zehn Jahren jedoch begannen wir den Wert dieser Entwicklung zu bezweifeln.
11. Unser Reichtum brachte offensichtlich nicht die erwünschte (wished-for) Lösung unserer Probleme."

26 The Barnhouse Effect

▼ *In Kurt Vonnegut's science fiction story "Report on the Barnhouse Effect" a young psychology instructor describes how Professor Barnhouse informs him about his discovery, a "force of mind" by which he can destroy anything he concentrates his thoughts on.*

Barnhouse scratched his head nervously. "I have never dared to concentrate as hard as I can for fear of the damage I might do." There was a depressing pause. "Up until a few days ago, I thought it best to keep my secret for fear of what use it might be put to," he continued. "Now I realize that I haven't any more right to it than a man has a right to own an atomic bomb."

He locked the laboratory door and drew the blinds, so that we were in twilight for a moment. "I'm odd, I know," he said. "It's fear of myself that's made me odd."

"I've found you somewhat eccentric, sir, perhaps, but certainly not ..."

"To give you an idea how crazy I am, I'll tell you what's been running through my mind when I should have been sleeping. I think maybe I can save the world!"

I have not heard from Professor Barnhouse since his disappearance a year and a half ago. Since that day, the professor has been systematically destroying the world's armaments, until there is now little with which to equip an army other than rocks and sharp sticks. His activities haven't exactly resulted in peace, but have rather caused a bloodless and entertaining sort of war. Every nation is flooded with enemy agents whose sole mission is to locate military equipment, which is promptly wrecked when it is brought to the professor's attention in the press.

1. *Explain the use, in lines 1–10, of*
   a) *the present perfect;*
   b) *the past tense.*
2. *Explain why in the second part of this passage (lines 11–18)*
   a) *the present perfect;*
   b) *the present tense are used.*
3. *Say what Professor Barnhouse did after he disappeared and what his activities led to.*

E Past Perfect – Simple and Continuous

27 Refresher Patterns

Past Perfect → **Past Tense**

1. I **had finished** nearly all my homework when my sister **came** in.
   I **had started** to read it through.
2. I **had been trying** to put the finishing touches to it when my sister **came** in.
   I **had been working** for 2 hours in all.

1. **past perfect simple:** to express what happened 2. **past perfect continuous:** to express what was in progress	before	an activity which occurred in the past. This activity may or may not be mentioned.

Note: For verbs which are usually not used in the continuous form, cf. RP, p. 9.

28 Who Had What?

Tom had had had, James had had had had.
Had had had had the teacher's approval.
Can you make sense of this statement? Try your luck by inserting inverted commas.

1.
"... and after I had closed my eyes, expecting him to kiss me, he ran off with my handbag."

2.
"I sent the boys to bed – they'd been fighting again!"

29 Friday the Thirteenth

Take the following infinitives and conjunctions to describe what happened to Mr Foster last month, on Friday the thirteenth. In each sentence use the past perfect in one clause, and the past in the other(s). Example:

the alarm clock – ring at four o'clock not set it properly	because

The alarm clock rang at four o'clock
because he had not set it properly.

1. get to the bus stop his bus – leave already	when
2. the next bus – be held up by the traffic have to wait another 27 minutes	as
3. arrive in his office his boss – ask for him several times	by the time
4. ask his secretary for a cup of tea bring coffee	although
5. dictate 13 letters into the dictaphone realize – be out of order	after
6. order rumpsteak for lunch be served fish	although
7. eat his salad find a dead fly in the salad dish	after
8. be about to pay for his lunch realize – forget his wallet	when
9. begin to rain discover – leave his umbrella in the restaurant	when
10. pay all his taxes find a reminder arrive home	although when
11. not be able to eat his soup at dinner his wife – put in too much salt	because
12. be asleep for half an hour his wife wake him up	after
13. she – want to tell him not take his sleeping-tablets	that

30 Love Story

1. *Here are some phrases which you will find useful for the picture story. Read and explain them:*

he: catch a first glimpse of s.o.
feel on top of the world
go down on one's knees
propose to s.o.
make a last desperate attempt
shed floods of tears
rush into s.o.'s arms

she: be hard-hearted
turn s.o. down
give s.o. the cold shoulder
give in to s.o.

2. *Say what Mr Murphy had tried and gone through before he succeeded in winning "her" hand (pictures 2–8). Use the past perfect – simple or continuous.*

1.

It was another boring evening with the inevitable book and the even more inevitable cup of tea.
But it had not always been like that! Mr Murphy's thoughts wandered back to how it had all begun ...

2.

3.

4.

5.

6.

7.

8.

9.

31 Cop and Robber

1. *Complete the following text using the past perfect – simple or continuous.*

Monday morning. Seven days after the million pound robbery at the General Post Office. Inspector Sharp is waiting in his car outside the gangsters' hiding place.

As far as Inspector Sharp could remember the sun (shine) when he first got there. But now it was raining so heavily and the skies were so depressingly dark that he felt as if it (pour) for days on end.

Sharp (sit) in his car watching the house for more than thirty minutes now. When he (arrive) a milk van (go) round a corner, fifty yards up the road from where he (park) the Triumph. Since then not a living soul (enter) the road.

He (not sleep) very well for nearly a week. He was tired and anxious, too, for he still hoped to catch Pistol Percy and his gang before they realized that he (discover) their hiding place. For two whole days he (spend) most of the time walking the streets of the neighbourhood. Once or twice he (look at) a map of the town. By Sunday night he (learn by heart) every street, every corner, every parking area within a mile of the gang's hiding place. There was not a sound to be heard except for the ticking of the clock in his car. He realized he (wait) for almost an hour now.

Sharp stretched restlessly in the seat and thought back to the time when Pistol Percy first (cross) his path. That (be) about seven years ago. At that time Pistol Percy (steal) cars and (sell) them to young people who didn't have a licence. Sharp (be given) the case. He …

▼ 2. *Go on with Sharp's recollections either by inventing your own plot or with the help of the following key words. Use the past perfect simple or continuous.*

Sharp … not very successful at first. For several weeks … but it was not until … one of Pistol Percy's young friends … At the final shoot-out Sharp himself … Pistol Percy … a five-year prison sentence. While … contact with a gang of bank robbers. After his release … his own gang … from car thefts to bank robbery … several good hauls. The most spectacular … General Post Office. Again Sharp … and after five days … hiding place which he was now watching.

32 Leaving Home

▼ *In James Joyce's short story "Eveline" we meet a young Irish girl, Eveline, who is planning to run away secretly with a young man, Frank. The following passage describes her thoughts and memories shortly before she leaves home:*

Home! She looked round the room, reviewing all its familiar objects which she had dusted once a week for so many years, wondering where on earth all the dust came from. Perhaps she would never see again those familiar objects from which she had never dreamed of being divided. And yet during all those years she had never found out the name of the priest whose yellowing photograph hung on the wall above the broken harmonium. He had been a school friend of her father.

She had consented to go away, to leave her home. Was that wise? She tried to weigh each side of the question. In her home anyway she had shelter and food; she had those whom she had known all her life about her. Of course she had to work hard, both in the house and at business.

She was to go away with Frank by the night-boat to be his wife and to live with him in Buenos Ayres, where he had a house waiting for her. How well she remembered the first time she had seen him. It seemed a few weeks ago. He was standing at the gate, his peaked cap pushed back on his head and his hair tumbled forward over a face of bronze. Then they had come to know each other.

First of all it had been an excitement for her to have a fellow and then she had begun to like him. He had tales of distant countries. He had started as a deck boy at a pound a month on a ship of the Allan Line going out to Canada. He told her the names of the ships he had been on and the names of the different services. He had sailed through the Straits of Magellan and he told her stories of the terrible Patagonians. He had fallen on his feet in Buenos Ayres, he said, and had come over to the old country just for a holiday. Of course, her father had found out the affair and had forbidden her to have anything to say to him.

"I know these sailor chaps," he had said.

One day he had quarrelled with Frank and after that she had to meet her lover secretly.

Annotations

to review to look consciously (and again) at – **shelter** security, protection – **peaked cap** Schirmmütze – **to tumble** to fall (down) untidily – **fellow** *here:* boyfriend – **Patagonian** native of the southern end of South America – **to fall on one's feet** to be fortunate – **chap** (coll.) young man

1. *We distinguish between the* plot, *i.e. the total sequence of actions presented in the thoughts, words and deeds of the characters in a dramatic or narrative work; and* flashbacks, *i.e. descriptions of events that happened before the point at which the story opens and the plot develops.*
   a) *Which actions (or thoughts) described in the text are part of the actual* plot? *Give examples.*
   b) *Which activities, circumstances or experiences described in the text are parts of* flashbacks? *Give examples.*
   c) *Which tenses are in most cases used for the presentation of the plot, which for the flashbacks*?

2. *Retell some of the things Eveline remembers about*
   a) *Frank's past;*
   b) *the develepment of their relationship.*

F Forms of the Future

33 Refresher Patterns

Future activities or states are expressed by various forms:

1. a) This year's school holidays **will** begin much earlier than usual. b) I'**ll** do my best to have everything ready in time. c) If we can manage, we'**ll** start around noon on the 23rd.	**shall/will** a) refers to external circumstances b) expresses willingness, promise, determination c) is used in main clauses before or after conditional and temporal clauses (cf. 5b)
2. a) We'**re going to** spend two weeks at the seaside along with Bob and his family. b) It's **going to** be great fun.	**to be going to** a) expresses a personal plan or intention b) expresses the speaker's certainty
3. Bob's **coming** here this evening.	**the present continuous** expresses an arrangement (usually with an adverbial of time)
4. He'**ll be calling** us up from his office. He'**ll be working** there up to 4.30.	**shall/will + continuous form** expresses what is expected to happen. It often extends over the whole of a period in the future.
5. a) Bob's bus **leaves** at 4.45 p.m. b) And if his bus **isn't** late, he'll be here before we **have** tea.	**the present simple** a) refers to timetable information b) is used in conditional and temporal clauses (cf. 1c)
6. He'**ll have left** his office by 4.40 p.m.	**the future perfect** expresses the completion of an activity in the future

1.

"Your husband will be down at half-past."

2.

"... and another thing – when are you going to fix this pram-handle?"

34 A Compromise

A telephone conversation between Mike, player and member of the committee of a local football club, and John, the club's coach:

M.: Hello John, is that you? It's me, Mike. Listen, I don't think I'll be coming this afternoon after all. You know we're leaving tomorrow morning for a holiday, and if I play this afternoon we won't get anything packed.

Hallo John, bist du's? Ich bin's, Mike. Hör mal, ich glaube, daß ich heute nachmittag doch nicht komme. Du weißt ja, wir fahren morgen früh weg in Urlaub, und wenn ich heute nachmittag spiele, kommen wir nicht zum Packen.

J.: Oh dear! I suppose you know that I'll have to rearrange the whole team if you don't come.

O je! Es dürfte dir klar sein, daß ich die ganze Mannschaft umstellen muß, wenn du nicht kommst.

M.: Try to see it from my point of view, John. Our train leaves at some unearthly hour tomorrow morning. If I don't help Emily this afternoon with the packing, she'll be hopping mad at me and our holiday will have been spoilt before it has even got started.

Versuch dich mal in meine Lage zu versetzen, John. Unser Zug fährt morgen in aller Herrgottsfrüh! Wenn ich Emily heute mittag nicht beim Packen helfe, ist sie stinksauer auf mich, und unsere Ferien sind schon verpfuscht, bevor sie angefangen haben.

J.: If you ask me, you'll make yourself

Wenn du mich fragst – du machst dich

very unpopular with the team, Mike, if you stay away. And what about the committee meeting after the match? Won't you be coming to that either?

M.: Oh, to hell with the committee! – Tell them I'm sorry, but I'm not going to make it this time.

J.: Now listen, Mike. I can just imagine their faces when I tell them you're not coming this afternoon. I'm dead certain you'll be dropped from the committee if you come along with a lame excuse.

M.: OK – I'm not going to argue with you. But I'll tell you what: When does the committee meeting start?

J.: We're meeting at five thirty.

M.: All right. – I'm going to start packing right now. I don't think I'll make it for the match – sorry, old boy – but here's what I'll do: I'll join you for the meeting. That way it'll be a compromise. Just tell the others what I told you. You'll do that for me, won't you?

J.: I'll have to, I suppose. I'll be seeing you at the meeting, then.

M.: Thank you, John. See you later.

sehr unbeliebt bei der Mannschaft, Mike, wenn du wegbleibst. Und was ist mit der Vorstandssitzung nach dem Spiel? Kommst du dazu auch nicht?

Ach, zum Teufel mit dem Vorstand! – Sag ihnen, daß es mir leid tut, aber ich schaff's diesmal nicht.

Jetzt hör' mal gut zu, Mike. Ich kann mir gut vorstellen, was sie für ein Gesicht machen, wenn sie hören, daß du heute nachmittag nicht kommst. Ich bin todsicher, daß du aus dem Vorstand fliegst, wenn du mit einer faulen Ausrede kommst.

Na ja, ich will jetzt nicht mit dir streiten. Aber paß mal auf: wann beginnt denn die Vorstandssitzung?

Wir treffen uns um halb sechs.

Schön. – Ich fange jetzt sofort mit dem Packen an. Ich glaube nicht, daß ich's bis zum Spiel schaffe – tut mir leid – aber ich mach's so: ich komme dann zur Sitzung. Das ist dann ein Kompromiß. Sag den andern einfach, was ich dir gesagt habe. Das machst du doch für mich?

Es bleibt mir wohl nichts anderes übrig. Ich seh' dich dann bei der Sitzung.

Vielen Dank, John. Bis später.

1. *Write down one example of each use of the future as explained in the Refresher Patterns, p. 41.*
2. *Explain the most striking difference in the use of the tenses in the English and German texts.*
3. **Translation**

Phrases like I don't think (that) *(cf. l. 2) are frequently followed by a form of the* shall/will *future. Note that many of these English phrases correspond to German adverbs, e.g. I suppose – "vermutlich".*
Here are some of them. Use them in the following translation.

I suppose	let's hope (I hope)	I assume
I expect (it's to be expected)	probably	I'm afraid
possibly	it's likely	I don't think (that)
I'm sure/certain		

a) Ich kann sicher heute nachmittag nicht kommen.
b) Bestimmt ist Emily sehr böse, wenn Mike ihr das Packen überläßt.
c) Vermutlich muß der Trainer die ganze Mannschaft vor dem Spiel umstellen.
d) Es ist zu erwarten, daß Arthur auch nicht kommt, wenn er erfährt, daß Mike nicht spielt.
e) Möglicherweise spielt Bill für ihn.
f) Hoffentlich schlagen wir sie trotzdem (all the same).
g) Ich glaube nicht, daß wir sie schlagen.
h) Wahrscheinlich gibt es ein Unentschieden (a draw).
i) Ich nehme an, wir verlieren das Spiel, wenn Mike und Arthur nicht kommen.
j) Leider muß ich jetzt aufhören.

35 Election Promises

Mr Weatherill, candidate for one of the opposition parties, has made some notes for an election speech:

1. build enough houses
2. improve social security
3. be envied for our social achievements
4. keep prices down once we have taken over
5. stop inflation one year from now
6. start our special committee work to restore economic stability next month
7. disclose new economic plans in the near future
8. restore law and order if you vote for us
9. reform taxation
10. even win this election by a large majority
11. convince everybody in this country by the time election day has come
12. lead this country back to her former greatness

At the election meeting Mr Weatherill says. "We ..." *Go on. Form complete sentences with the phrases given above. Use suitable forms of the future. Use more than one form if possible.*

36 Holiday on the Moon

In the following exercise connect the sentences with the conjunctions given in the margin. Use the future with will *where possible.*

You want to spend your holidays on the moon? This is what it will be like:

1. You are much safer in your spacecraft than on the roads. — although
   You are a bit frightened.
2. The space hostess serves you the first delicious space lunch. — as soon as
   You are no longer afraid.
3. You land at the 'spaceport'. — when
   You do not appreciate the beauty of the moon.
4. You do not see anything at all. — because
   There is all the hustle of getting into your space suit.
5. You arrive at the 'astrotel'. — after
   You probably want to see the earth.
6. You want to see a 'full earth'. — if
   You must wait for the middle of the night on the moon.
7. You want to enjoy the sunshine on the moon. — if
   You hardly see the earth at all.
8. You go for a walk. — whenever
   You have to wear your space suit.
9. You put it on. — after
   You are isolated in your own environment.
10. You are not allowed out of your hotel. — unless
    You go with someone else.
11. You do not get lost. — because
    The porter at the hotel keeps in touch with you through your helmet radio.
12. You get lost. — if
    They can easily locate you by radio.
13. You sit on the moon's surface and gaze around. — when
    You feel 'on top of the world'.
14. You experience this solitude for a while. — after
    You probably feel an aching desire to go home.
15. On your return to the earth you are glad to be home again. — but
    You never forget your holiday on the moon.

Annotations

hustle [hʌsl] quick and restless activity – **astrotel** from astra (*Latin:* stars) + hotel – **aching** *here:* intense

37 Foul Future

"Listen, I'm not thinking of myself. If you send me off the field I shall be suspended and United will have to play without me. They'll lose their matches and the number of spectators at home matches will fall catastrophically. And the money that would have been spent on admission will be spent in the shops and cause inflationary pressure, so that prices will rise. This will, of course, spread to other towns, to your town; and your wife will find that her housekeeping money won't go as far as it did, and she'll ask you for more. And when you tell her that you've no more to give she'll say 'There's nothing we can do, then, but take in lodgers.' And one of your lodgers will be an attractive commercial traveller with a roving eye, and one day you'll come home to find ..."

Annotations

to be suspended to be forbidden to play for a period of time – **admission** entrance (to a match) – **lodger** someone who pays money to live in a room in another person's house – **roving** wandering

Say what – according to the player – will have happened by the end of his suspension, if it takes place,

a) *to his club,*

b) *to the national economy,*

c) *to the referee and his wife,*

d) *to himself.*

38 The Star

Miss Vivian Jay, the well-known film star, is about to leave for America. Some newspaper reporters have been waiting for her at the airport, hoping to get an interview.
Fill in suitable forms of the future (cf. Refresher Patterns, p. 41). Use more than one form if possible.

Reporter: Miss Jay, would you mind answering a few questions, please?

Miss Jay: Gentlemen, my plane (leave) in half an hour. So if you don't mind I (answer) a few questions only.

Reporter: You (make) another film in Hollywood?

Miss Jay: I hope so. But everything depends on Mike Hitch, the producer. I (meet) him tonight and I'm sure a decision (be made). If everything (work out) all right, we probably (shoot) the first scenes by this time next month.

Reporter: What about Don Ryan? He (be) your partner?

Miss Jay: Certainly not! I (not work) with him again after last year's fiasco.

Reporter: What you (do) if Don Ryan has already got the part?

Miss Jay: I (return) to England right away.

Reporter: A question about your private life. You (see) your ex-fiancé in Hollywood?

Miss Jay: Why not? I bet he (wait) for me at the airport when I (get) there.

Reporter: Do you think that you (get together) again?

Miss Jay: I'm afraid I (have to go) now. My plane (take off) in 20 minutes.

39 There'll be Peace

In J. B. Priestley's play An Inspector Calls *the Birlings are celebrating the engagement of Sheila Birling to Gerald Croft. On this occasion Mr Birling, Sheila's father, makes a speech. It is an evening in spring, 1912.*

Birling: Gerald, I'm going to tell you frankly that your engagement to Sheila means a tremendous lot to me. She'll make you happy, and I'm sure you'll make her happy. I hope it won't be too long before you're married ... When you marry, you'll be marrying at a very good time. Yes, a very good time – and soon it'll be an even better time.

Eric (Sheila's brother): What about war?

Birling: Glad you mentioned it, Eric. I'm coming to that. Just because the Kaiser makes a speech or two, or a few German officers have too much to drink and begin talking nonsense, you'll hear some people say that war's inevitable. And to that I say – fiddlesticks! The Germans don't want war. Nobody wants war. There isn't a chance of war. The world's developing so fast that it'll make war impossible. Look at the progress we are making. In a year or two we'll have aeroplanes that will be able to go anywhere. And look at the way the automobile's making headway – bigger and faster all the time. And then ships. Why, a friend of mine went over this new liner last week – the *Titanic* – she sails next week – forty-six thousand eight hundred tons – New York in five days – and every luxury – and unsinkable, absolutely unsinkable. That's why you've got to keep your eye on facts like that, progress like that – and not a few German officers talking nonsense ... And remember what I'm telling you now. In twenty or thirty years' time – let's say, in 1940, – you'll be giving a little party like this – your son or daughter might be getting engaged – and I tell you by that time you'll be living in a world that'll have forgotten all these silly little war scares. There'll be peace and prosperity and rapid progress everywhere.

Adapted from *An Inspector Calls*, by J. B. Priestley. Reprinted by permission of A. D. Peters & Co Ltd.

Annotations

a tremendous lot very much, a great deal – **the Kaiser** Kaiser Wilhelm II. – **fiddlesticks**! nonsense! – **to make headway** to make progress – **liner** passenger ship belonging to a steamship line – **Titanic** [tai'tænik] She was the largest ship of that time. On her maiden voyage she collided with an iceberg in April 1912. Nearly 1,500 persons were drowned. – **war scare** fear that war is about to start

1. *Explain the following forms of the future which are taken from the text (cf. Refresher Patterns, p. 41):*

l. 1	I'm going to tell you	l. 20	you'll be giving a little party
3	When you marry	21/22	you'll be living
15	she sails next week	22	that'll have forgotten

2. a) *Birling makes a lot of predictions using* will. *Which of them concern the future development of the world?*
   b) *What makes him do this, and what does this tell us about his character?*
3. *The play was first produced in 1946. Describe the possible effect of Birling's predictions on audiences of 1947 or today.*

Modal Auxiliaries

A Can – May – Must and Equivalent Forms

40 Refresher Patterns

Herr Gerber, the guide of a group of German tourists, and Mr Dibley, a member of the London Tourist Board, are discussing the group's plans.

Do you think we **can** go to Downing Street before lunch?	I'll find out when lunch is being served and then I'll **be able to** tell you. But I'm afraid it won't **be possible** for you **to** go near No 10. Recently tourists haven't **been allowed to** go near the Prime Minister's residence for security reasons.

can	to be able to:	ability
	it is possible to (that):	possibility (circumstances make it possible)
	to be allowed (permitted):	permission

May we take photographs in the British Museum? So it **may (might)** be better to leave them in the bus.	I'm sure you won't **be allowed** to take your cameras into the exhibition room. That will **perhaps** be the best idea.

may	to be allowed (permitted):	permission (very polite)
	perhaps:	possibility (the speaker considers it possible)

When **must** we be back for lunch? Let's find him. He **must** be at the reception desk now.	Sorry, but I'll first **have to** talk to the manager of the hotel. **I'm sure** we'll find him there.

must	to have to:	obligation, necessity
	to be sure (certain):	certainty (the speaker considers it certain)

1.
"Don't pretend you can't hear your wife calling you, Charlie. I can hear your knees knocking!"

2.
"Don't count your winnings yet, Fred – there may be an objection to this one."

3.
"There must be *other* ways of teaching him to be a good watch dog!"

41 Travelling to Britain

In 1947 it wasn't normally possible for Germans to travel abroad, but I was offered a scholarship at a British university and was therefore one of the first Germans to be allowed to visit Britain after the war.

As I wasn't permitted to buy any foreign currency, I had to pack enough food and drink for the two-day journey before I left Munich. I changed trains five times en route to Calais and every time I had to grab my luggage and drag it up and down platforms and finally on and off the Channel boat.

At Dover I wasn't allowed to go on to London with the other passengers. "I'm afraid you can't go on yet," said the immigration officer. "We must ring up the Foreign Office first, and you might have to wait a while. If you think your friends at the university might be worried, you may use my telephone."

In the end I had to wait about four hours before the authorities finally let me in. Then, on the train to London, the engine broke down and there was a further delay before I was able to continue my journey. All in all it must have taken me some sixty hours to reach my destination.

Nowadays, travellers from Germany can reach most places in Britain within a few hours. They can fly to London from most German cities and there might even be direct flights to Manchester or Glasgow. It can take less time from Frankfurt to London by plane than from Frankfurt to Stuttgart by train.

At the airport passengers can buy duty-free cigarettes, spirits and perfume and during the flight they may be served dinner or a snack, depending on the time of day. All they have to do with their luggage is to hand it over to the airline people.

Today a supersonic airliner can fly round the earth in less time than it took me to travel from the Continent to Britain.

1. *Find the modal auxiliaries or the equivalent forms used in the text and explain what they express. Example:* wasn't possible *in line 1 expresses* possibility *(cf. Refresher Patterns, p. 49)*
2. *Complete the following sentences by using the modal auxiliaries or the equivalent forms given in the Refresher Patterns, p. 49. Give all possible versions.*

Today travellers	**Just after the war** they	**In future** they
a) … reach England within hours.	… spend hours and hours on trains.	… reach England in less than an hour.
b) … easily return to Germany on the same day.	… have had to spend another day or even two to return to the Continent.	… have breakfast at home and be back from London for lunch.
c) … enter the United Kingdom without a visa.	… not … visit the United Kingdom without a visa.	… no longer need a passport.
d) … face different problems: strikes, traffic jams, strict controls, etc.	… get to know fellow travellers quite well because of the long journey.	will hardly … establish personal contacts during the short trip.

42 Explosion

1. *The following extracts are taken from a live radio report on an explosion at a chemical plant. Insert* can, can't *or* may, might.

a) I'm afraid we … give you any details about the catastrophe at the moment.
b) At present we … get hold of anyone to give us further information which … throw more light on the situation.
c) We … be able to talk to a member of a rescue team later on, though.
d) This … be possible when the first rescue squad is relieved in about fifteen minutes.

e) A moment ago we were able to talk to Chief Engineer Bradley. He says he ... give us the exact number of victims, which ... well be more than the twelve dead who were discovered immediately.
f) He thinks there ... still be some men in Hall IV who ... escape because they are trapped by the heat and the smoke.
g) They ... have to send in another rescue squad if the workers ... get out themselves.
h) I ... see some men now carrying stretchers to the ambulances. We'll try to get over to them as they ... know more about what is happening.

▼ 2. *Say what must be done in this situation or what else may (might) happen at the scene of the catastrophe. Make use of the following key words:*

a) further explosions
b) panic
c) roads leading to the plant
d) more rescue squads
e) first aid stations
f) poisonous gases
g) evacuation
h) hospitals

43 Permission or Ability?

1. At a party Mat O'Leary had had too much to drink. He was staggering about, bumping into everybody and had already knocked down a vase and two flowerpots. Suddenly he caught sight of the hostess carrying a tray full of drinks.
"Hullo, baby," Mat rolled towards her. "Can I take one?"
"You may if you can," she replied.

2. An amateur group once wanted to produce and act a play by George Bernard Shaw. They wrote to the great man, asking: "Can we produce your play 'Pygmalion'?" Shaw's answer was brief: "You can't, but you may."

B May – Must Not; Must – Need Not

44 Refresher Patterns

Daughter: **May** I have the car this afternoon, Daddy? *Father:* Yes, you **may.**	But you **mustn't** drive too fast.
permission	prohibition
Daughter: **Must** I be back for tea-time? *Father:* You **must** be back for supper.	But you **needn't** be back for tea-time.
obligation/necessity	absence of obligation/necessity

Note: *may not* expressing prohibition is used

a) in short answers to questions like "**May I** ...?" "No, you **may not.**"

b) in official notices (Cars **may not** be parked on the pavement).

"Darling, may we have the car tonight?"

45 British Consuls

Look at the following list of phrases and say what a British Consul abroad must, must not, need not *be or do:*

1. offer advice to British citizens abroad
2. be in his office day and night
3. contradict the official policy of his government
4. keep in touch with his Embassy
5. cause scandals
6. be a nobleman
7. break the laws of the host country
8. show intelligence, ability and common sense
9. play bridge or cricket
10. promote British trade
11. transact business to his own advantage
12. pay for cocktail parties from his own pocket
13. be married
14. interfere in the politics of the country where he is Consul
15. protect his countrymen in times of crisis
16. be a secret service agent

46 Touring by Kayak (Translation)

▼ Eine Gruppe Schulkinder und ihr Leiter (guide), Peter Martin, sind auf einer Kajak-Tour. Bevor sie losfahren, stellen ihm die Kinder einige Fragen:

1. *Frank:* Dürfen wir heute nachmittag baden gehen, wenn wir im Lager ankommen?
2. *Mr Martin:* Ja. Aber ihr dürft nicht allein gehen. Und ihr müßt mir sagen, wo ich euch finden kann.
3. *Irene:* Michael sagte, daß wir nicht die ganze Zeit Schwimmwesten tragen müssen?
4. *Mr Martin:* Natürlich braucht ihr sie nicht die ganze Zeit zu tragen, aber ihr dürft nicht vergessen, sie anzulegen, wenn ihr in die Boote steigt.
5. *Oliver:* Dürfen wir das Lager verlassen und uns die Umgebung ansehen?
6. *Mr Martin:* Ja. Aber nach Anbruch der Dunkelheit (after dark) dürft ihr nicht weggehen.
7. *Ellen:* Müssen wir unser Gepäck zu den Booten bringen?

8. *Mr Martin:* Alles Gepäck kann im Kombi (station wagon) gelassen werden. Ihr braucht nichts in den Booten mitzunehmen.
9. *Walter:* Müssen wir auf dem Fluß in einer Reihe fahren (keep in line)?
10. *Mr Martin:* Nein. Aber ihr müßt in Sichtweite (within sight of each other) bleiben. Das ist vielleicht nicht immer leicht, aber ihr dürft nicht zu weit zurückfallen.

47 Show Jumping

1.

"Competitors must enter the arena on horse back."

2.

"But they must not start until the signal is given."

3.

"Only three refusals are permitted

4.

and unauthorised assistance is prohibited."

Write out two new versions of each caption using forms given in the Refresher Patterns, p. 53.
Example: 1. Competitors *must not* lead their horses into the arena.

C "sollen"

48 Refresher Patterns

1. The Ambassador **is said to** have been kidnapped.	**to be said to** is used to express that someone is passing on information that he has heard
2. Mrs Baker, who lives near the Embassy, says to her husband: "Wait a minute! That must have been the black car I saw. **Shall** I tell the police about it?"	**shall** (with *I* and *we*) is used to introduce a question about a person's wishes
3. a) *Mr Baker:* "Yes, of course. Anyone who has observed anything **is to** tell the police at once." b) *Mrs Baker:* "The kidnappers must have known that the Ambassador **was to** leave the house at that time."	**to be to** is used a) to pass on an instruction b) to express an arrangement
4. a) *Mr Baker:* "That's why I keep saying that ambassadors **should** have bodyguards." b) *Mrs Baker:* "The police **ought to** have watched the Embassy more closely."	**should/ought to** are used to express that something is advisable or a (moral) obligation

1.
"There's been a revolution. – I'm to free you, and you're to execute me!"

2.
"Well, you should insist they give you your fortnight in summer like everyone else."

49 Road Safety (Translation)

1. Während der letzten drei Jahre soll die Zahl der Verkehrsunfälle (road accident) in den meisten Ländern zurückgegangen sein.
2. Trotz dieser Entwicklung sollte man sich mit den gegenwärtigen Verhältnissen nicht zufriedengeben.
3. Was sollte getan werden? Vor allem sollte die Industrie sicherere Wagen bauen.
4. Jeder Wagen sollte eine genormte Sicherheitsausstattung haben.
5. Das wird vielleicht die Preise erhöhen, wird aber notwendig sein, wenn irgendein Fortschritt möglich gemacht werden soll.
6. In seinem Buch *The Four-wheeled Death Trap* schreibt Ronald Weene: „Es sollte 30 Jahre dauern, bis gute Sicherheitsgurte (safety belt) auf den Markt gebracht wurden. Aber die Frage ist jetzt: Soll es weitere 30 Jahre dauern, bis alle Fahrer sie regelmäßig benutzen?"
7. Vor fünf Jahren schlugen Ärzte in Schweden vor, daß Erste Hilfe in jeder Schule unterrichtet werden sollte, und heute soll das Land bereits 80% seiner Schulen mit besonderen Ausbildungszentren (training centre) ausgestattet haben.
8. Sollen wir die Sicherheit auf den Straßen (road safety) dem Zufall überlassen, oder sollten wir nicht endlich etwas dafür tun?

50 Join the Queue

Use should, ought to *or a form of* to be to *to complete the following text. Give all possible versions.*

No visitor to London ... miss the Houses of Parliament. You ... know, however, that if you arrive any time after twelve o'clock, there'll be a queue. This ... not come as a surprise to anyone who knows what attraction the "Mother of Parliaments" still has for many Britons.

When I was in London last time, I went to Westminster just after lunch. The visitors ... be let in at two o'clock, the session ... begin at half past. You ... have seen the queue! I really ... have turned on my heel and gone away.

Well, I joined the queue, because I ... write an article about that day's debate in the school-magazine. And I was looking forward to it, as someone had told me that the Prime Minister himself ... speak.

When, finally, it was two o'clock and the doors ... be opened, an official appeared and told us that the session ... not ... take place after all. One might think that people ... have protested. But they didn't!

D Mixed Exercises

51 Before the Exam

Before her examination in German, Jennifer has an interview with Mr Cullers, her professor.–Find out which of the three forms given in the margin comes closest to the meaning of the auxiliary in the text. Use it to form an alternative version of the original sentence.

J.: **May** I ask you some questions, sir?	Shall I – Must I – Can I
C.: Yes, of course.	
J.: **Can** you give me any hints about the exam questions?	Should you – Is it possible for you – Are you to
C.: Of course I **can't** give you any details.	I needn't – I might not – I'm not allowed to
However, you **ought to** go over the material that we covered this term.	you should – you may – you can
You **needn't** go back any further.	You can't – You don't have to – You shouldn't
J.: **Are** we **to** use the German or the English grammar terms?	Do we have to – Might we – Can we
C.: I'm afraid you **must** know both the German and the English terminology.	you should – you'll perhaps – you'll have to
There **may** be questions which refer to both.	There should be – There can be – There'll perhaps be
J.: A friend of mine told me that we'**d be allowed to** use a dictionary.	we must – we should – we could
But she **couldn't** tell me whether this was the case for all parts of the exam.	she wasn't able to – she wasn't allowed to – she wasn't to
C.: The latest regulations say that dictionaries **may not** be used in any kind of language test.	mustn't – needn't – shouldn't
J.: But she was quite sure about it.	
Shall I find out where she got it from?	Am I to – Do you want me to – May I
C.: You **needn't** waste your time.	You don't have to – You mustn't – You may not
The new regulations came out this morning. They **might** even be on the bulletin board already.	They ought to be – They are perhaps – They can be
J.: Thank you, Professor Cullers.	
C.: Please remember you **are not to** take any books into the exam room.	you aren't able to – you needn't – you mustn't

52 Scuba Divers

1. *Complete the following text by using suitable auxiliaries.*

Anybody ... become a Scuba diver. Quite close to the coastline lies a whole world of flora and fauna, coral and wrecks, a silent paradise available to the explorer, the photographer or just the enterprising holiday-maker. Some people ... merely wish to dive for their own salad lobster.

Scuba divers ... have very different social backgrounds. They ... not be rich or upper class; and they ... not be particularly tough either. But every beginner ... start by learning how to use the mask and breathing tube.

He ... not spend a lot of money on the equipment, because much of it ... be hired. But if he wants to, he ... also buy it from a specialist dealer.

There are not many rules, but they ... be observed. The most important one is that you ... never hold your breath during ascent, as this ... cause your lungs to collapse. Secondly, you ... never ascend faster than 60 feet per minute. But if you observe these rules, Scuba diving ... be one of the most exciting adventures.

Adapted from *Multiple Choice Questions in English*, by John Eynon. © 1970 John Eynon, St. George's Press, Hamish Hamilton Ltd, London.

Annotations

Scuba Self-Contained Underwater Breathing Apparatus (Preßluft-Tauchgerät) – **lobster** Hummer – **breathing tube** Atemschlauch – **equipment** things needed for an activity – **ascent (to ascend)** upward movement

2. a) *Say why people may want to become Scuba divers.*
   b) *What does the text say about the kind of people who want to be Scuba divers?*
   c) *Say what rules Scuba divers must observe.*

53 The Super Jumbo

I'*m sure* you've read the ads which tell us that the Super Jumbo is the airplane of the future. It *is said to* carry more than 600 passengers at one flight.

"You *needn't* worry," Rudolph Hammilfinger, the designer of the Super Jumbo told me in the course of an interview the other day. "We'll *be able to* get her up and going."

"What worries me," I said, "is that there isn't an airport in the country that *can* handle an airplane of that size."

"That isn't my problem," Hammilfinger said angrily. "I just build the airplane."

"That's wonderful, sir," I said, "but *shouldn't* there be some thought given to situations that *might* arise when you are loading and disgorging more than 600 passengers at the same time?"

"That's a problem the airline companies will *have to* deal with," he said. "You *ought to* talk to them."

"How will you *be able to* handle the passengers on those new enlarged planes?" I asked Rodney Clover, the president of Jam-Packed Airlines.

"The airports will *have to* worry about that. All we *have to* do is to see that more and more people fly."

I said, "It seems to me that unless you *are able to* manage the ground problems, you *shouldn't* be flying those big planes."

"All I *can* say is, we ordered them, we paid for them, and we are going to fly them. The people you *should* speak to are the airport authorities. They *ought to* know what to do with the planes when they land."

"It *might* be better to speak with the Federal Aviation Authority," Timothy Merryweather, the spokesman for the Airport Managers Association told me. "They *are said to* be working on what to do with the big planes."

An FAA representative pointed out that they *couldn't* do anything about it unless Congress authorized enough funds to enlarge airports.

I dutifully went over to Congress – but they weren't in session. It was just as well. They would *perhaps* have sent me back to Rudolph Hammilfinger.

Adapted from *The Establishment is Alive and Well in Washington*, by Art Buchwald. © by permission of the author.

Annotations

to disgorge to throw up or out as from the throat – **Federal Aviation Authority** Bundesluftfahrtbehörde – **it was just as well** there was no need for regret

1. *Say which "modality" is expressed by the italicized forms; cf. the Refresher Patterns of chapters A (p. 49), B (p. 53), C (p. 56).*

▼ 2. *Satire is a form of writing which ridicules the imperfections of man, society, certain ideas, etc. It uses the laughter which it provokes as a weapon to bring about a change for the better.*

   a) *Which attitude is ridiculed in the text?*

   b) *Which sentences with modal auxiliaries or equivalent forms illustrate this attitude?*

   c) *Which modal auxiliaries does the author use to point out to the people he interviews that they have forgotten some important factors?*

Reported Speech

54 Refresher Patterns

In January 1976 Alexander Snow started on a 15,000-mile walk from South to North America. Ten months later, in Peru, Snow **told** a reporter (that)

1. he **had started** from near Cape Horn ten months before. (i.e. *before* he talked to the reporter)	**past perfect**
2. he still **felt** very fit. (i.e. *at the time* he was talking to the reporter)	**past tense**
3. he **would arrive** in Alaska in two years' time. (i.e. *after* he talked to the reporter)	**future in the past**
4. Mr Snow said that walking **keeps** a person fit. (Mr Snow said: "Walking keeps a person fit.")	The **tense** used in direct speech is **maintained** if the speaker states a fact which is generally accepted as true.

Note: If the introductory verb is in the present tense, the present perfect or the future tense, the same tenses are used in reported speech as in direct speech:
e.g. He says he is feeling fine.
He has always wondered why people are afraid of physical exercise.
He will no doubt be wondering why the others are tired out.

1.
"You never told me your brother had a smashing train set like this, Jean!"

2.
"I was wondering when you'd turn up!"

55 "0 Table"

Before being admitted to Eton, Winston Churchill was interviewed by a Latin master of that famous public school.

"You have never done any Latin before, have you?" the teacher started his interview.

"No, sir."

"This is a Latin grammar," the teacher explained, opening the book at a page covered with strange words.

"You must learn this," he decided pointing to a list of peculiarly arranged words. "I'll be back in half an hour and see what you know."

And there was Churchill, trying to face the first declension of Latin nouns:

mensa	a table	mensae	of a table
mensa	0 table	mensae	to or for a table
mensam	a table	mensa	by, with or from a table

There was one thing, of course, he could always do: learn it by heart. And so he did.

"Have you learned it?" the master asked, when he returned.

"I think I can *say* it, sir," Winston replied.

The master seemed to be satisfied, which encouraged Churchill to ask the decisive fundamental question:

"What does it mean, sir?"

"It means what it says. *Mensa*, a table. *Mensa* is a noun of the first declension. There are five declensions. You have learned the singular of the first declension."

"Then why does *mensa* also mean '0 table', and what does '0 table' mean?" Churchill continued to argue.

"*Mensa*, 0 table, is the vocative case," the teacher tried to explain.

"But why is it '0 table'?" Churchill wanted to know.

"You would use it in speaking to a table," the teacher said.

"But I never do," the troublesome boy protested.

"If you are impertinent, you will be punished severely," the master concluded this memorable interview.

Annotations

declension Deklination – **vocative case** Vokativ: Fall der Anrede i. Lat. – **troublesome** causing troubles – **impertinent** not showing proper respect

Change the sentences in direct speech into reported speech using the following introductory clauses:
The teacher asked him (l. 3); Churchill answered (l. 5); The teacher explained (l. 6); He told Churchill (l. 8); He informed him (l. 9); The master asked (l. 16); Winston replied (l. 17); Churhill inquired (l. 20); The teacher gave him to understand (ll. 21/22); Churchill wanted to know (l. 23); The teacher tried to explain (l. 25); The boy wanted to know (l.26); The teacher pointed out (l.27); Winston protested (l. 28); The teacher retorted (l. 29).

56 How to Lose Weight

Last summer I decided to go on a crash diet guaranteed to make me lose 20 pounds in a month.

I must say that the first day was fine. Although I fainted twice, I managed to get through the day by going to bed at eight. The next morning my wife insisted that an egg with breakfast wouldn't hurt me, and since she is wiser than I am (she weighs only 119) I assumed she knew what she was talking about.

At noon I lunched with a friend who told me I was only kidding myself. He said that meat is more fattening than potatoes. I have always respected this friend's judgement (on the same occasion he casually mentioned that he had just made another million in the stock market), so I had potatoes with my meat.

In the evening I dined at the home of a wine dealer. He was shocked when I said that I wouldn't drink any wine with my dinner. He pointed out that wine is a great digestive aid and unless I digested my food correctly it would automatically turn to fat. It made sense, and I had a half bottle of a very extraordinary and honest Burgundy.

On the third day another friend told me that the best way to lose weight is to eat nothing but starches. He insisted his brother-in-law had lost ten pounds that way. I've always been fond of spaghetti, and I had a bowl for lunch just to see if his brother-in-law knew what he was talking about.

One evening my wife reported that her hairdresser swore that fresh lobster or shrimp or crabmeat were non-fattening. She said she couldn't remember which one I liked and that this was why she had bought all three. I couldn't remember either, so I ate all of them.

I'm still continuing the crash program. And if you can take a word of advice let me tell you that the main thing is not to do it alone. You need friends. If it weren't for the people who have encouraged me already, I don't think I would ever make it.

Adapted from *The Art Buchwald Crash Diet Plan*, by Art Buchwald. © Food and Fitness 1973, The Blue Cross Association, Chicago.

Annotations

crash diet Intensivdiät – **to kid oneself** to deceive/fool oneself – **casually** making it seem unimportant – **stock market** Aktienmarkt – **digestive** Verdauungs- – **starches** carbohydrates – **bowl** [bəul] dish or big plate – **lobster** Hummer – **shrimp** Krabbe (Garnele) – **crabmeat** Fleisch von Krebsen

1. *Go over the text and pick out all sentences with reported speech. Say whether the actions in the clauses with reported speech take place*
   a) *before*
   b) *at the time* } *the author makes these statements (cf. RP, p. 62).*
   c) *after*
2. *Say in which clauses with reported speech the tenses of direct speech are maintained (cf. RP, p. 62, 4 and Note).*
3. *Change the following sentences from the text into direct speech:*
   a) I must say that the first day was fine.
   b) My wife insisted that an egg with breakfast wouldn't hurt me.
   c) A friend told me I was only kidding myself.
   d) He pointed out that wine is a great digestive aid.
   e) He insisted his brother-in-law had lost ten pounds that way.
   f) My wife reported that her hairdresser swore fresh lobster was non-fattening.

57 Plane Crash in the Canadian Wilderness

On the flight back from his fur trading post at Great Bear Lake, Jim Kane's plane was caught in a snowstorm and crashed. Kane was injured but miraculously survived the next six weeks until he was rescued. A radio reporter interviewed him during a press conference at St. Patrick's Hospital, Providence:

Interviewer: Mr Kane, you've just gone through a medical check-up. How do you feel and what did the doctors say?

Jim Kane: My injured leg still hurts and I'm still a bit shaky, of course. I think I lost about 40 pounds.

Interviewer: No one can imagine how you survived those six weeks. Did you have any food on board?

Jim Kane: As I could hardly move the first two days I couldn't get at the emergency rations which I always keep on board. Later I recovered three or four tins from the wreckage.

Interviewer: How long did they last?

Jim Kane: I made them last about two weeks, I guess.

Interviewer: And what did you eat afterwards?

Jim Kane: There were days when I didn't eat anything at all, as far as I can remember. Some days I crawled to nearby trees and scratched off the bark to chew it. Later I caught a squirrel.

Interviewer: Did you have any firearms with you?

Jim Kane: There had been two guns on the plane, but I didn't find them in the wreckage. That's why I should recommend any pilot to carry a firearm and some rations on him. I'll never climb into a plane with empty pockets again.

Interviewer: Does this mean you'll go back to your old job up at Great Bear Lake?

Jim Kane: I'll stay in hospital for at least two more weeks before I spend some time with friends in Vancouver. In spring I hope to return to the site of the crash to recover some of the furs and what's left of the plane. Meanwhile I'll have plenty of time to think about my job.

Annotations

fur soft, thick hair of certain animals – **shaky** weak, unsteady – **emergency ration** [i'mə:dʒənsi 'ræʃn] fixed quantity of food set aside for situations when normal food supplies are not available – **bark** outer covering on the trunk and branches of trees – **to recover** *here*: to get back (s.th. lost etc.)

1. *Later the radio reporter told a colleague who had missed the press conference all about the interview. Put the interview into reported speech with the introductory clauses in the past tense:* I *mentioned* that Kane had just gone through a medical check-up and *asked* him how he…

2. **A Newspaper Report**

   Still a bit shaky and minus 40 pounds, Jim Kane, the fur trader from Great Bear Lake, gave his first press conference at St. Patrick's Hospital yesterday. Kane told the reporters …

   Continue this newspaper report by summarizing the interview. Include sentences with reported speech where suitable.

Note: say/tell ("sagen") in reported speech:

1. a) He **said** that he had caught a squirrel.
   If the person spoken to is not mentioned, *say* must be used.

1. b) He **said to the interviewer** that he had caught a squirrel.
   If the person spoken to is mentioned after *say*, *to* must be used.

2. He **told the interviewer** that he had caught a squirrel.
   Tell must be followed by the person addressed. It is never used with *to*.

58 He Who Laughs Last Laughs Longest

The Camerons and their guests were passing the time before dinner was served: Mr Cameron told them what had happened to him one afternoon.

1.

He said that ...
smoke a cigar
dream of a holiday on the Bahamas

2.

He added that ...
not notice a banana skin
slip and fall flat on his back
still have a swollen ankle

3.

Then Mr Price described what had happened to him on a Sunday afternoon, when he had gone fishing. He told them that ... He continued that ...
wait for hours for a fish to bite
slide down the river-bank and to splash into the water
still have a cold
buy his fish at the fishmonger's in future

4.

Mrs Dawson told them what had happened to her and her husband. Her story was that ...
paint their dining-room
stand on top of the ladder
lose their balance
plunge headfirst from the ladder and land in the paint with a splash
still be black and blue all over

5.

6.

The guests were roaring with laughter when Mr Wilkinson started to describe his and his wife's misfortune. He said that …

walk down the staircase
miss a step
give his wife a kick
go flying through the air
still look for one of the parcels
never go down the staircase together with his wife

Their laughter came to a sudden end when Rose, the Camerons' housemaid, opened the door and, laughing her head off, told them that …

trip over her own feet
drop the whole bloody dinner
not be any dinner tonight

59 The Witness

Mr Birch is suspected of having murdered his wife. After his arrest Mrs Davies, the cashier of a camping ground in the Black Hills, USA, is interrogated as a witness. Fill in the correct verbal forms.

Mr Clifford, the District Attorney, showed the witness a photo and asked her whether she (ever see) the man before. Of course she (see) him, was the prompt reply.

(be) she absolutely sure, the Attorney inquired. Mrs Davies hesitated for a moment but then firmly declared that she (not think) she (be mistaken).

Why, then, she (not become suspicious) when Birch (leave) the camping ground on the evening in question without his wife, Mr Clifford demanded. To this the witness answered that she (not know for sure) on that evening whether he (enter) the ground alone or in company. But that she (now remember) that upon arriving at the ground Birch (ask) his wife for some small cash, as she, Mrs Davies, hadn't been able to change the 50 dollar bill he had offered her.

When asked whether she (feel) that she (be able) to identify the man from a group of suspects, Mrs Davies replied that she (help) the police in whatever way she (can). But then she wanted to know whether this (be possible) without being seen herself.

The District Attorney assured her that they (put) her seat in a darkened room so that the man (not recognize) her.

60 The Betrayed Revolution

1. The following is an extract from George Orwell's political satire *Animal Farm.* Under the leadership of the pigs the animals of the Manor Farm successfully rebel against their human masters. However they lose their freedom again when the pigs turn into brutal dictators. After an inspection of Animal Farm Mr Pilkington, a farmer, and Napoleon, one of the pigs – who during the animals' rebellion had been deadly enemies – together with their friends are celebrating their fraternization and the suppression of the "lower animals". Mr Pilkington makes a speech which is cheered enthusiastically. Then Napoleon speaks.

Fill in the correct verbal forms.

When the cheering had died down, Napoleon, who had remained on his feet, intimated that he too (have) a few words to say.

Like all of Napoleon's speeches, it was short and to the point. He too, he said, (be happy) that the period of misunderstanding (be at an end). For a long time there (be) rumours – circulated, he had reason to think, by some malignant enemy – that there (be) something subversive and even revolutionary in the outlook of himself and his colleagues. They (be credited) with attempting to stir up rebellion among the animals on neighbouring farms. Nothing (can) be further from the truth! Their sole wish, now and in the past, (be) to live at peace and in normal business relations with their neighbours. This farm which he (have) the honour to control, he added, (be) a cooperative enterprise. The title-deeds, which (be) in his own possession, (be owned) by the pigs jointly.

He (not believe), he said, that any of the old suspicions still (linger), but certain changes (be made) recently in the routine of the farm which should have the effect of promoting confidence still further. Hitherto the animals on the farm (have) a rather foolish custom of addressing one another as "Comrade". This was to be suppressed. There (also be) a very strange custom, whose origin was unknown, of marching every Sunday morning past a boar's skull which was nailed to a post in the garden. This, too, (be suppressed), and the skull (already be buried). His visitors might have observed, too, the green flag which flew from the masthead. If so, they would perhaps have noted that the white hoof and horn with which it had previously been marked (now be removed). It (be) a plain green flag from now onwards.

He (have) only one criticism, he said, to make of Mr Pilkington's excellent and neighbourly speech. Mr Pilkington (refer) throughout to "Animal Farm". He (cannot) of course know – for he, Napoleon, was only now for the first time announcing it – that the name "Animal Farm" (be abolished). Henceforward, the farm was to be known as the "Manor Farm" – which, he (believe), was its correct and original name.

From *Animal Farm*, by George Orwell.

Annotations

title-deed document of s.o.'s property – **to promote** to encourage and increase – **boar** a male pig – **skull** Schädel

2. *Use reported speech to answer these questions.*
   What did Napoleon say about
   a) "the old suspicions";
   b) the recent changes on Animal Farm;
   c) the names "Animal Farm" and the "Manor Farm"?

61 Disarmament

Once upon a time, all the animals in the zoos decided that they would disarm, and they arranged to have a conference to settle the matter. So the Rhinoceros said, when he opened the proceedings, that the use of teeth was barbarous and horrible and ought to be strictly prohibited by general consent. Horns, which were mainly defensive weapons, would, of course, have to be allowed.

The Buffalo, the Stag, the Porcupine, and even the little Hedgehog, all said they would vote with the Rhino. But the Lion and Tiger took a different view. They defended teeth, and even claws, which they described as honourable weapons of immortal antiquity. The Panther, the Leopard, the Puma, and the whole tribe of small cats all supported the Lion and the Tiger.

Then the Bear spoke. He proposed that both teeth and horns should be banned and never used again for fighting by any animal. It would be quite enough if animals were allowed to give each other a good hug when they quarreled. No one could object to that. It was so fraternal and that would be a great step toward peace. However, all the other animals were very offended with the Bear, and the Turkey fell into a perfect panic.

The discussion got so hot and angry that all those animals began thinking so much about horns and teeth and hugging when they argued about the peaceful intentions that had brought them together, that they began to look at one another in a very nasty way.

Luckily, the keepers were able to calm them to go back quietly to their cages and they began to feel quite friendly with one another again.

From *The Churchill Wit*, by Bill Adler. Coward, McCann & Geoghegan, Inc., New York 1965.

Annotations
stag Hirsch – **porcupine** ['pɔ:kjupain] Stachelschwein – **hedgehog** Igel – **leopard** ['lepəd] – **turkey** Truthahn – **claw** Kralle – **to hug** umarmen

▼ 1. *Retell the fable; use reported speech where possible.*

2. a) *Say which arguments the Lion, the Tiger and "the whole tribe of small cats" brought up to express their disapproval of the Rhino's views and add further arguments to support the cats' standpoint. Use reported speech.*

b) *Say which arguments are brought up by the other animals to counter the Bear's suggestion. Use reported speech.*

Conditional Sentences

62 Refresher Patterns

Seventeen-year-old Jane is reading the advertisements in the morning paper.

1. *Jane*: Listen to this, Dad: If you **want** to be rich tomorrow, If you **send** us your address,	**write** to us today. we**'ll** tell you more.	The condition may be fulfilled
if-clause: **present tense**	main clause: **imperative** or **future**	
2. a) *Father*: OK, write to them, and if you **should** get rich,	**don't forget** your Dad. you **won't/wouldn't** have to work any more.	It is left open whether the condition will be fulfilled, but it is less likely
if-clause: **should**	main clause: **imperative/future/conditional**	
2. b) If you **were to** make the slightest profit,	I **would** be the first to congratulate you.	
if-clause: **were to**	main clause: **conditional**	
3. *Father*: Believe me, if you **answered** an ad like that, If I **were** you,	you **would** make yourself ridiculous. I **wouldn't** even bother to write.	It is most unlikely or impossible for the condition to be fulfilled
if-clause: **past tense**	main clause: **conditional**	
4. *Jane:* If you **had seen** an ad like this thirty years ago, And if you **had answered** it,	you **would have answered** it, too. maybe we **would** be better off now.	The condition was not fulfilled
if-clause: **past perfect**	main clause: **conditional perfect/conditional**	

63 If . . .

1. a) On one occasion, George Bernard Shaw sent Churchill two tickets for the opening night of his new play. "And bring a friend, if you have one," Shaw wrote.
   Churchill regretted that he was otherwise engaged on that evening, but wrote to Shaw: "Please send two tickets for the second performance, if there is one."
   b) Lady Astor once told Churchill: "If you were my husband, I'd poison your coffee."
   Churchill replied: "If you were my wife, I'd drink it."

   Adapted form *The Churchill Wit*, by Bill Adler. Coward, McCann, & Geoghegan, Inc., New York 1965

2. *Explain what types of conditions are expressed by the verbal forms used in the conditional sentences (cf. RP, p. 72).*

64 How to Talk to a Big Boss

Nigel Stafford, a hopeful young actor, is trying to persuade Arthur Milligan, a theatre director, to give him a contract. Mr Milligan, however, is not quite sure that Stafford is the right man for his company.

Stafford: a) "If you give me a contract, you won't regret it."
b) "If you gave me a chance, I wouldn't disappoint you."
c) "If you'd seen me play Hamlet, you wouldn't hesitate."

Go on arguing like Nigel. Use the following phrases to form conditional sentences like the ones given above.

1. give me an audition	see for yourself
2. not be so young	be offered lots of contracts
3. watch me performing	be convinced
4. try me out now	hire me on the spot
5. be ill last winter	even have appeared on TV
6. read the critics' reviews	realize how good I am
7. ask my former director	recommend me
8. be fatter	get the part of Falstaff at Stratford
9. give me the part of Macbeth	be a great success
10. say "Yes"	turn down all other offers

65 Lucky Andrew

Andrew White, who expects to inherit some money from an uncle, is already speculating on what to do with it. So he makes this list:

1. savings account	10 to 15% interest
2. stock market	fortune
3. car	seaside
4. holiday	Hawaii
5. fashionable clothes	social prestige
6. party at the Hilton	event of the year
7. children's home	name in the newspapers
8. yacht	success with the girls
9. Aero Club	pilot's licence
10. debts	clear conscience

"Well," Andrew says to himself, "now let's see what I could do with the money:
1. If I opened a savings account, I would/could/might earn 10 to 15% interest.
Go on, using conditional sentences.

66 Chain Reaction or: A Theory of Aggression

1. If Mrs Nelson had not lost her temper with her husband, he would not have scolded his son. If Mr Nelson had not scolded his son, he ... *Go on.*
2. *Give the story a "moral". Begin with* "If ...".

67 Uncle Harry the Great

Uncle Harry is telling his nephew what he could/would have achieved in his life, or what he could/would still achieve if he wanted to:

a) "If I had handed in my application in time, I'd have got a scholarship."

b) "I could win huge sums of money in TV quizzes if I cared to."

Go on. Use the following phrases to form conditional sentences like the ones given above:

1. climb Mount Everest long ago
   find the right team
2. sail round the world one of these days
   not suffer from sea-sickness
3. not break my leg in 1960
   win a gold medal in the Olympics
4. become a concert pianist before the year is out
   be more ambitious
5. learn several foreign languages even now
   not be busy doing other things
6. not have so much other work to do
   get a professorship at Oxford next term
7. be more friendly with the boss and his wife
   be top manager of Transatlantic Motors soon
8. not prefer my freedom as a young man
   marry a millionaire's only daughter
9. make a fortune on the Stock Exchange
   buy oil shares five years ago
10. tell you more
    not have to leave now

68 Socrates in Paris

1. *Fill in the correct verbal forms:*

If Socrates, 469–399 B.C., (come) to life in Paris in 1776, many things (seem) strange to him; but he (not have) much trouble in making himself at home there. Assuming he had learned the French language, he (be able) to take up his former occupation of going about and asking his fellow citizens puzzling questions concerning the nature of truth and virtue.

But if Benjamin Franklin (enter) Philadelphia today, he (be) less at home in his own home town after two hundred years than Socrates (be) in Paris after two thousand years. He (recognize) Independence Hall, if he (stumble) upon it, but he (not know) where to look for it at first. He (not know) how to use a telephone, or what it was that made automobiles go. It might well be that, if he (see) this noisy, crowded city, he (prefer) to return to his silent grave.

Adapted from *History of Modern Europe, Course One.* United States Armed Forces Institute, Madison, Wisconsin.

2. a) *Which types of conditional sentences are used in the text?*
   b) *Why are conditional sentences of type 1 (cf. RP p. 72) not used in the text?*

69 **The Population Explosion** (Translation)

Vocabulary Aids:

family planning	developing countries	population explosion
birth control	food problem	birth rate
overcrowded	underpopulated area	

▼ **Translation:**

1. Gegenwärtig verdoppelt sich die Weltbevölkerung alle 35 Jahre. Wenn dies 900 Jahre lang [so] weiterginge, dann gäbe es etwa 60.000.000.000.000.000 (sixty thousand billion) Menschen auf der Erde.
2. Was würde passieren, wenn die Bevölkerung in dieser Weise weiterwachsen würde?
3. Etwa 100 Menschen würden auf jedem Quadratmeter der Erdoberfläche (the earth's surface) leben, und wenn nicht alle Länder Familienplanung und Geburtenkontrolle anwenden, dann wird eine Katastrophe unvermeidlich werden.
4. Selbst wenn Wissenschaftler eine Möglichkeit finden sollten, den Überschuß an Menschen (surplus people) auf andere Planeten zu schicken, würde es nur etwa 200 Jahre dauern, bis sie so überfüllt wären wie die Erde.
5. Doch wir brauchen nicht Jahrhunderte vorauszuschauen (look ahead), wenn wir herausfinden wollen, wo das Problem liegt.
6. Es wird immer mehr Hunger in den Entwicklungsländern geben. Selbst wenn es möglich sein sollte, das Ernährungsproblem zu lösen, wird der Mangel an Raum die Feindseligkeit unter den Menschen verstärken (increase hostility), wenn die unbewohnten Gebiete nicht bewohnbar gemacht werden können.
7. Wenn in den letzten 20 Jahren alle Länder die Bevölkerungsexplosion so wirksam (efficiently) bekämpft hätten wie Japan, das seine Geburtsrate halbiert hat, wäre es vielleicht noch möglich gewesen, das Problem zu lösen.

70 Meet Mr Custer

Fill in the correct verbal forms:

If Mr Custer (realize) that St Peter had watched him approaching the Heavenly Gates, and if he (notice) that Peter had turned the key twice, he probably (be) more careful in choosing his words. But as it was, still feeling the self-made millionaire and self-assured businessman he had been in his long and successful life, he burst out: "Well, I (be) damned if it (not be) Old Pete, just the man I've been looking for! Custer's the name. Custer of the Denver Custer Computer Company, the greatest in its field, if you (get) what I mean."

If Mr Custer (be) of a more sensitive nature, he (see) the look of disgust on St Peter's face, but never having been in doubt for a moment as to the charm of his personality he merrily continued, "Well, old man, if I (be) you, I (ring) the bells. It's Bill Custer, come to brighten the place up!"

It took St Peter the better part of half an hour to get Mr Custer to understand that if he (believe) that he was qualified to enter Heaven, he (have to) give proof of the good deeds he had done on earth. "If your record (meet) the entrance re-

"He's only the third this week –
we'll have to lower the standards if this goes on."

quirements, we (give) your application due consideration," St Peter concluded his explanation.

"By Jove!" Mr Custer grumbled, if this place (be run) more efficiently, you (have) all the records at the ready when a customer arrives. If I (be) still alive, I (sell) you our latest CC TX 7 model – just press the button and, zoom, there you are: all the records you could possibly want. But if you (insist), well, here is a good deed I remember."

And so Mr Custer told St Peter the story of how he had once, and against all his principles, bought a box of matches from an old beggar and when the man hadn't been able to give him back two cents for the nickel he had received from Custer – the price for the matches was three cents – he had told him to keep the change. "If that (not be) a good deed," Custer concluded triumphantly, "I (not know) what is!"

St Peter turned to St Michael who keeps the book of the good and evil deeds of all men on earth. "See whether you can find any record of this gentleman's story," he said to his assistant. "And if what he says (be) true, (give) him back his nickel and (tell) him to go to Hell!"

Annotations

disgust strong disapproval – **record** facts known about a person's past – **requirement** necessary condition – **due** adequate, proper – **nickel** a US five cent coin

71 The Dilemma

The hero of Erskine Caldwell's short story Horse Thief *is a rather naive but very loyal farm-hand. Leaving his girl-friend Naomi Moseley one very dark night, he by mistake takes the horse belonging to her father, Lud Moseley. As a result he is sent to jail as a horse thief. There, in a rather confused state of mind, he thinks over his position:*

I reckon I could worm out of it some-way, if I made up my mind to do it. But I don't like to do things like that. It would put Naomi in a bad way, because if I said I was there seeing her, and had put Betsy in the stall to keep her quiet, and took Lightfoot out by mistake in the dark when I got ready to leave – well, it would just look bad, that's all.

Lud Moseley has been telling people as how he is going to send me away for twenty years so he can get Naomi married to that widowed farmer who runs twenty plows, and maybe he will get me sent away sure enough before Naomi gets a chance to tell what she knows is true.

But somehow, I don't know if she'll say it if she *does* get the chance, and I have been thinking that maybe Naomi might not come right out and tell what she knows after all.

I'd come right out and explain to the Sheriff how the mixup happened, but I sort of hate to mention Naomi's name in the mess. If it had been a Sunday night, instead of night before last, a Thursday, I could – well, it would just sound too bad, that's all.

If Naomi comes to town and tells what she knows, I won't say a word to stop her, because that'll mean she's willing to say it and marry me. But if she stays at home, and lets Lud Moseley and that widowed farmer send me away for twenty years, I'll just have to go, that's all.

I always told Naomi I'd do anything in the world for her, and I reckon this will be the time when I've got to prove whether I'm a man of my word, or not.[1]

Annotations

Naomi ['neiəmi] – **Moseley** ['məuzli] – **plow** [plau] AE Pflug – **to come right out** to tell the truth openly

1. *Use conditional sentences to say what will happen, would happen or would have happened*

   a) if the "horse thief" tells the Sheriff what really happened;
   b) if Naomi had at once agreed to tell what she knew;
   c) if she refused to tell the true story;
   d) if Lud Moseley should learn the truth;
   e) if Naomi refused to marry the widowed farmer;
   f) if the Sheriff doesn't accept the young people's story;
   g) if the hero decides to be "a man of his word";
   h) if he had tried to escape from prison;
   i) if he were sent away for twenty years;
   j) if Lud Moseley forgave the young people.

▼ 2. *What does the frequent use of conditional sentences by the narrator-hero tell us about his way of thinking?*

[1] Caldwell's story ends here. He leaves the reader to find his own solution to the "horse thief's" dilemma.

The Passive Voice

72 Refresher Patterns

The passive voice is mostly used in texts such as instructions for use, technical, scientific, historical descriptions and newspaper reports. (In German sometimes the active voice with "man".)

1. a) Scrabble is a game which **is played** in many countries. b) It can **be played** *by two, three or four players.*	The passive voice is preferred when the doer is self-evident, unimportant or unknown. A by-agent is only used if it seems necessary to give information about the doer.
2. At the beginning of the game *each player* **is given** seven letters, with which he has to make up words.	Unlike their German equivalents certain English verbs can form the passive voice with a personal subject (cf. list 1, p. 87).
3. A dictionary may **be referred to** when the spelling of a word causes trouble.	Prepositions which are closely connected with verbs remain with these verbs in the passive voice (cf. list below).

e.g. deal with	look after	rely on
dream of	look (up)on s.o. as	send for
hear of	make use of	speak about/of/to
laugh at	pay for	talk of/to
listen to	refer to	take care of

"That's another lie! I wasn't expelled – I resigned!"

73 **Art Thefts Reach £6 Million** (A Newspaper Report)

Scotland Yard still seems to have made little progress in the case of the ten valuable paintings, which were stolen from the London home of Lord Gimmingham last Sunday. Although a description of the missing paintings was sent to every port and airport in Britain within 24 hours after the theft had been discovered by a caretaker, it is believed that the pictures have already been smuggled out of the country.

At today's press conference at the Yard journalists were handed photographs of the stolen paintings. In a statement by a Yard spokesman three similar art thefts were referred to, all of which have taken place since the beginning of the year. The total loss resulting from all four thefts is estimated at £6 million. It was announced that photographs of the paintings would be shown on the evening news.

1. a) *Say in which different tenses the passive voice is used.*
   b) *Find one example each for the use of the passive voice as described in the Refresher Patterns, p. 80.*
2. *What had happened before the journalist wrote this article?*
   Ten valuable paintings had been stolen from ...
3. *What usually happens when such an event occurs?*
   The police are called in ...
   Key words: insurance; experts; press; TV; rewards.
4. *What else may / might / can / could happen to a stolen picture?*
   a) It ... abroad
   b) Another picture ... over the original
   c) ... remove from its frame
   d) ... by an unsuspecting art lover in Australia
   e) ... hide ...
   f) ... never ... again

74 **Being Discriminated Against**

"Have you ever been glanced at and hated in one minute? Or talked to and not really been talked to as a person? Have you entered a room and immediately felt those walls go up?"

From an article in an American school magazine

We have all experienced discrimination in one form or another. Say which people *may be discriminated against and use the following expressions to explain how this may happen.*
Example: talk to – *Teenagers are* often *talked to* as if they were small children.

1. point at
2. not listen to
3. stare at
4. look down upon as inferior
5. refer to as a burden
6. look (up)on with contempt
7. laugh at
8. look down upon
9. make fun of
10. not think of as equals

75 "Mysterious Stranger" Still Missing (Translation)

▼ *In your translation of the following extracts from a newspaper report use the passive voice where possible. Keep in mind that in English personal subjects are often preferred to non-personal subjects in passive sentences.*

1. Der elfjährige Sam Anderson weiß noch nicht, ob er die £3000 behalten darf, die ihm vor einer Woche von dem „mysteriösen Fremden" gegeben wurden.
2. Hinsichtlich (as to) der Herkunft des Geldes machte man gestern bei Scotland Yard der Presse gegenüber nur vage Andeutungen (offer vague theories).
3. Wie letzte Woche berichtet wurde, hatte sich ein „ausländisch aussehender Fremder" dem Jungen im Hyde Park genähert.
4. Der Mann war ihm einige Minuten lang gefolgt, bevor er ihm schließlich die Tasche mit dem Geld übergab.
5. Kurz danach sah man den Mann aus dem Park laufen.
6. Inzwischen hat man Sam Photos mehrerer verdächtiger Personen (suspects) gezeigt.
7. Bei der Pressekonferenz sagte Sams Vater, Mr James Anderson, daß man über seinen Jungen gelacht habe, als er die Geschichte zum erstenmal erzählte.
8. Nach dem, was (from what) man ihm bei Scotland Yard mitgeteilt hatte, konnte Mr Anderson nicht sagen, ob Sam der volle Betrag ausbezahlt (pay) werde oder nicht.
9. Man riet ihm, einen Rechtsanwalt zu nehmen (consult a lawyer).
10. „Wir hoffen, daß man den ‚mysteriösen Fremden' noch findet", sagte Sams Vater.

76 Looking for a Quiet Place

One sunny morning Mr Patterson goes to St James's Park to read his newspaper in peace. He sits down on a bench, but soon he …
Complete the following story. Use the passive voice where possible and the by-agent where necessary.

1.

join
draw into a conversation

2.

not leave in peace
annoy

3.

frighten
jump on

4.

hit
bark at

5.

attract

6.

interrupt
yell at

77 To the Moon and Back - In Two and a Half Seconds

One of the many purposes which a laser may be put to is the measurement of very long distances. The distance between particular places on the earth and on the moon, for example, can be measured by the time it takes a laser beam to travel from the earth to the moon and back – roughly two and a half seconds. Here is an extract from a report about the transportation of reflectors to the moon and the observation of the signals which were obtained from the reflectors.

The Apollo reflector panel was placed on the lunar surface by astronauts Amstrong and Aldrin on 21 July 1969. Attempts were made almost immediately to obtain range measurements, but these were hampered by the brief time available before the moon became too low in the sky on that night. Further delays were caused by weather problems, but on 1 August the Lick Observatory succeeded in obtaining strong return signals from the Apollo 11 reflector and in measuring the difference between the observed and predicted range with an accuracy of 7 meters. Soon afterward, return signals were obtained with a high confidence level at McDonald also. Successful range measurements to the Apollo 11 reflector have also been reported by observatories in Arizona, in France and in Japan.

Four additional reflector panels have been placed at other locations on the lunar surface since 1969. The first was a French-built package of 14 glass corner reflectors, carried to the moon by the Soviet spacecraft Luna 17 in November 1970. The package was mounted on the eight-wheeled lunar exploration vehicle Lunakhod 1. Return signals from it have been observed by a Soviet group at the Crimean Astrophysical Observatory and by a French group at the Pic du Midi Observatory. No observed returns have been reported since the first few months after landing, and the reflector thus may have been coated with dust stirred up during surface explorations.

From *The Lunar Laser Ranging Experiment*, Bender, P.L. et al, *Science*, Vol. 182, pp. 229–238, 19 October 1973.

Annotations

laser apparatus for the amplification and concentration of light waves into an intense light beam – **Apollo** *here:* Apollo 11 (first manned landing on the moon) – **panel** Platte, Tafel – **range** distance – **to hamper** to hinder – **to predict** to tell beforehand – **with a high confidence level** von hoher Zuverlässigkeit – **McDonald** name of an observatory of the University of Texas – **corner reflector** Winkelspiegel, Winkelreflektor – **to mount** to instal, to set up – **Crimean** [krai'miən] – **to coat** to cover

1. *Use the passive voice where possible to answer these questions:*
   a) *To which purpose was a laser put in the experiments described in the text?*
   b) *How were these experiments carried out?*
   c) *Where were return signals from the moon received?*

2. *Explain the frequent use of passive sentences in the text (cf. RP, p. 80).*

3. *When astronauts travel in space the gravity of the earth has no hold upon them. Use the following phrases to say what* cannot *and what* must be done *in a weightless spacecraft.*
   a) overcome problems of weightlessness
   b) rely on one's normal sense of gravity
   c) wear magnetic shoes
   d) make use of guide-ropes
   e) deal with the difficulties of weightless eating
   f) take food and drink in the customary way
   g) cook meals
   h) pour liquids into cups
   i) keep liquids in plastic tubes
   j) squeeze drinks from tubes into the mouth
   k) use ordinary spoons
   l) fasten down all objects firmly

Verbs and their Objects

A Verbs with a Direct Object and an Indirect Object with or without "to"

78 Refresher Patterns

1. Verbs with an indirect object with or without "to" (cf. list 1)

a) The teacher	gives	**Bob**	the book.
Basic word order:		indirect object	direct object

But:

b) The teacher	gives	the book	**to Bob** (and not **to Dick**)
		direct object;	the indirect object is stressed
c) The teacher	gives	it	**to him.**
		direct and	indirect object are pronouns
d) The teacher	gives	the book	**to the pupil who has to prepare a report.**
			The indirect object is much longer than the direct object.

2. Verbs with an indirect object always with "to" (cf. list 2)

a) The teacher	explains	the rule	**to the pupils.**
Basic word order:		direct object	indirect object

b) The teacher	explains	**to the pupils**	the ways of using the book.
			The direct object is stressed and/or is much longer than the indirect object.

3. Verbs with an indirect object never with "to" (cf. list 3)

Bob	asks	**the teacher**	a question.
The word order is		indirect object	direct object

1.	award	give	lend	pass	sell	teach
	bring	grant	offer	pay	send	tell
	deny	hand	owe	promise	show	
2.	announce	describe	entrust	mean	repeat	
	deliver	dictate	explain	mention	say	
	demonstrate	distribute	introduce	propose	suggest	
3.	ask	envy	take (e.g. It took him two hours.)			refuse
	cost	forgive	save (e.g. It saved me a lot of work.)			

1.

"Normally I wouldn't give her such a big, expensive gift but this is our Silver Wedding."

2.

"Show it to all the girls at the office first, Mabel, then we'll sell it and get married."

79 Pop Festival

Insert the objects given in brackets with or without to.

1. Shortly before the concert began, Dirk Bogal, the festival manager, announced (the audience/the news that Glenn Allen wouldn't be able to perform).
2. He tried to explain (the disappointed fans/the reasons)
3. But it took (him/fully ten minutes) to make his voice heard above the uproar.
4. When he offered (them/a different programme) he was booed down.
5. The audience's anger was quite understandable as the tickets had cost (them/a small fortune).
6. It was not until he handed (Dolly Person, who was the festival's other star/the microphone) that the audience quieted down.
7. The evening was saved when she told (them/the story of her partnership with Allen).
8. This meant she was repeating (her admirers/what most of them knew already).

9. For instance, that Allen had never once refused (her/his personal encouragement and help).
10. In fact, she described (her listeners/ the situation), calling it a unique opportunity to demonstrate (the absent star/her gratitude).
11. Then she introduced (the audience/her latest hits).
12. In the end even the Glenn Allen fans gave (her/a standing ovation).

80 "Explaining Creatures"

In the opening passage of his novel *Mr Sammler's Planet* Saul Bellow says that "intellectual man had become an explaining creature". He continues: "Fathers to children, wives to husbands, lecturers to listeners, experts to laymen, colleagues to colleagues, doctors to patients, man to his own soul, explained."

1. *Say what the "explaining creatures" in the above quotation usually explain to the people mentioned in the text. Add the following objects:*

a) fathers:	the things they have learned in their lives
b) wives:	the reasons for wanting to be more emancipated
c) lecturers:	their ideas
d) experts:	the functioning of complicated systems
e) colleagues:	plans
f) doctors:	symptoms
g) man:	his wishes, hopes and fears

▼ 2. *What do the following people communicate to other people? Use two objects in your answers.*

a) Tourist guides show ...
b) Politicians deliver ...
c) Dictators deny ...
d) Priests offer ...
e) Scientists suggest ...
f) Teachers explain ...
g) Salesmen introduce ...
h) Grandparents tell ...
i) Little children ask ...

81 False or Not?

In town one day I remembered that my wife had asked me to get her some fruit. I bought some oranges in a fruit-store and wanted to pay for them with a ten-dollar bill, which I laid on the counter.

Insert the objects given in brackets with or without to.

1. The owner immediately called his wife and showed (her/the bill).
2. "Oh, it's back again!" she laughed. Her husband explained (me/her reaction).
3. The owner showed (his customers, who were now looking on with amused interest/some obvious faults in the bill).
4. I handed back (the man, who was smiling at me in sympathy/the oranges). At that point I quietly left the store.
5. At home I told (Melinda/the story).
6. "That bill!" she exclaimed. "Well, somebody gave (me/it) and, I'm afraid, I passed .... on ... (you/it)."
7. It didn't take (Melinda/a minute) to think of a way out. She went to her friend Gloria and said (her): "I promise (you/half the amount) if you get rid of the bill for me."
8. Two days later Gloria handed (Melinda/a perfectly good five-dollar bill).
9. Some time later Melinda found the ten-dollar bill in her purse again and once more suggested (Gloria/the same deal).
10. When the wretched bill turned up a third time, I told (a friend of mine who works in a bank/the story).
11. "Bring (me/it)," he said. "I'd like to see it."
12. When he had examined the bill, he said (me/this): "You could have saved (yourself/a lot of trouble) if you had come to me at once. There are defects in the printing, I grant (you/that). But the bill is not false."
13. He put it with some others and gave (me/two five-dollar bills).

82 The Pension

In his autobiography, the Irish writer Frank O'Connor describes his father's passionate interest in filling out forms which the British Government sent him every year. The authorities wanted him to prove that he was still alive and therefore had the right to receive a pension.

He explained the problem carefully to Mother while he considered how best to handle it. When the form was filled out and in its envelope on the mantelpiece, and Mother had been warned that she must post it with her own hand and not entrust it to me, he would become emotional again about the goodness of the British Government and its consideration for its old servants. The pension meant much more to him than the trifle of money it represented. It gave him a personal interest in the British Government. A Liberal Government might be good for the Irish cause, but a Conservative one would be better for the pension. It gave him wild dreams, because no quarter passed without his toying with the idea of compounding it for a capital sum, the size of which staggered imagination. It gave him the prospect of a happy old age.

Abridged from *An Only Child*, by Frank O'Connor. Reprinted by permission of A.D. Peters & Co Ltd.

Annotations

mantelpiece Kaminsims – **consideration** thoughtful attention to the wishes, feeling or needs of others – **trifle** a small amount – **quarter** three months – **to compound one's pension** to give up a regular pension in favour of one single payment – **to stagger** to shake

1. *Find the verbs with two objects and explain the sentence structures (cf. RP, p. 86).*
2. *To answer the following questions take the verbs used in these questions or those given in brackets. Use two objects in each answer.*
   a) Who did Mr O'Connor explain the problem to?
   b) How might the government have reacted if Mr O'Connor had ever forgotten to fill out the forms? (deny)
   c) What did Mr O'Connor tell Frank's mother not to do? (entrust)
   d) What significance did the pension have in Mr O'Connor's life? (mean, give)
   e) What did the pension demonstrate to Mr O'Connor about the British Government?
   f) What chances did a compounding of the pension offer Mr O'Connor?
   g) Why do you think the author includes this story of his father's pension in his autobiography? (describe)

B Verbs with a Direct Object and an Object Complement

83 Refresher Patterns

1. The managing director regarded Gerald Smith **as** one of his best men.	**object complement with "as"** acknowledge regard look (up)on think of recognize
2. He had always considered him (as) a possible candidate for the management	**object complement with or without "as"** choose elect consider
3. That is why he made him his personal assistant.	**object complement without "as"** appoint declare call make crown

Note: When the verb is in the passive voice, the direct object becomes the subject of the sentence, e.g. **He** *was made personal assistant.*

1.

"We mustn't look on this as just another holiday romance, Miss Newson, promise me you'll write."

2.

"So they've made you captain of the darts team! What do I do now – get down on my knees?"

84 The Violent End of Non-violence (Translation)

▼ *For the verbs in italics cf. RP, p. 91.*

1. In den sechziger Jahren *galt* Martin Luther King *als* der bedeutendste Führer der schwarzen Bürgerrechtsbewegung (Civil Rights Movement) in den USA.
2. Er wurde als Sohn eines Baptistenpfarrers (Baptist minister) 1929 in Atlanta geboren (be born the son of).
3. King *betrachtete* Gandhis Philosophie der Gewaltlosigkeit *als* die stärkste Waffe im Kampf der Schwarzen um gleiche Rechte.
4. Im Jahre 1955 *wählte* ihn die Bürgerrechtsbewegung von Montgomery, Alabama, *zu* ihrem Führer.
5. Sein Erfolg in Alabama *machte* King bald *zum* Sprecher (spokesman) der Schwarzen Amerikas.
6. King *hielt* sit-ins und Protestmärsche *für* die wirksamsten Mittel der Gewaltlosigkeit.
7. Er *erklärte* den Kreuzzug (crusade) gegen Diskriminierung und Armut *zum* höchsten Ziel der Bürgerrechtsbewegung.
8. Manche Weiße *hielten* ihn *für* einen Kommunisten, und manche Schwarze verachteten (look down upon) ihn als Verräter.
9. Trotzdem *erkannten* ihn immer mehr Schwarze *als* den überzeugendsten Vertreter ihrer Interessen an.
10. King starb als Märtyrer (die a martyr). Seine Ermordung im Jahre 1968 wurde von der Mehrheit der Amerikaner *als* eine nationale Schande (disgrace) *betrachtet.*

85 Political Views

1. *Say what some opponents of a modern democratic system of government think about it.*
   Use the object complements given on the right.

a) They declare parliamentary democracy ...	an uncritical herd of voters
b) They look (up)on reformers ...	a system of weakness
c) They call the people ...	sacred rights
d) They regard class privileges ...	radicals

2. *Say what some people think of the masses.*
Use the object complements given on the right
In their opinion the masses . . .

a) regard ready-made ideologies ...	their representatives
b) make charlatans ...	their own political programmes
c) choose attractive-looking candidates ...	heroic figures
d) think of Presidents ...	their leaders

▼ 3. *Say what* you *think all responsible citizens of a democracy should do.*
Insert suitable adjectives + nouns.

a) They should make ... their leaders.
b) They should choose ... their representatives.
c) They should elect ... their Prime Minister.
d) They should recognize ... the most important aspect of democracy.
e) They should regard ... basic to democracy.
f) They should look (up)on ... a danger to democracy.

Non-finite Forms of the Verb

A Infinitive Structures

86 Refresher Patterns

The manager of an English hockey club helps a visiting German team to find their way about:

1. I'll tell you	how	to find	your way around.
verb	**question word**	**infinitive with "to"**	

The structure expresses what can, must, should be done.

2. a) I'll have	Stephen	show	you the showers.
I'll make	him	get	everything ready.
b) He'll let	you	have	the keys.
verb	**direct object**	**infinitive without "to"**	

The structure expresses what someone is
a) asked or ordered to do ("veranlassen");
b) allowed to do ("zulassen").

3. a) I expect	him	to be	here any moment.
verb	**direct object**	**infinitive with "to"**	

The structure expresses what is expected, caused or allowed; cf. list 1. below.

3. b) I should prefer	you	to put away	your things first.
verb(al) expression	**direct object**	**infinitive with "to"**	

The structure expresses a wish or its opposite; cf. list 2 below.

1. allow	permit	2. want
ask	require	hate
cause	get, order	wish
advise	tell	should like/prefer/hate
expect	warn (not to)	

1.

"You certainly know how to train gun-dogs!"

2.

"You mean to say you called me in from play, and made me wash my face and hands for *this*?"

87 Sheriff Brewster or the Alligators?

Neither for our parents nor for us children had there ever been any question where to spend our holidays. Year after year it was Lone Star Bay, Florida, a paradise in those days. And that meant Joe Brandell.

Joe was a retired coast guard who made us believe that his sole purpose in life was to turn our holidays into one glorious adventure.

Whenever we set out on an "expedition" up Peacock River he would let us have his fishing equipment with harpoon and everything. Sometimes he even got Daniel, an ever-grumbling old Negro who lived with him, to dig for worms, which he had him put in an old can with wet soil "to keep them tasty".

Joe used to show us how we ought to row the boat upstream, and where we could get closest to those big pelicans fishing along the banks. And he never forgot to tell us when we had to return with the outgoing tide. In fact, he knew very well how to impress certain warnings on our carefree, young minds: "I expect you to be back before sundown. I should hate you to spend the night among those alligators out there. You surely don't want me to get the Sheriff and a search party out of bed in the middle of the night!"

The idea of Sheriff Brewster, a bull-necked, red-haired ruffian, coming after us made us tremble with fear and at the same time decide to be back on time. I guess we should have preferred the alligators to follow our boat all night long to Brewster and his men coming to get us.

Eileen Stewart

1. *Explain the use of the infinitive structures (cf. RP, p. 94).*
2. *Which feelings and reactions did the existence of Joe Brandell and Sheriff Brewster cause in the children*? It made them …
3. *What did Joe teach the children so that their "expeditions" would be a success?* He taught them …
4. *What were Joe's warnings?* He warned them …

88 Learning to Ski

Skiing can be fun, but it has to be taught properly. It all depends on how good your instructor is. Complete the following sentences by filling in (to) you *as object + an infinitive. Put the question word* how *before the infinitive where necessary.*

The good instructor

1. He shows … stand properly on skis.
2. He explains … fasten the bindings.
3. He always warns … lift your sticks too high.
4. He has … practise on easy slopes at the beginning.
5. He tells … keep your balance.
6. He makes … feel confident.
7. He prefers … take your time.
8. He lets … have a rest when you need one.
9. He never orders … go on when you are tired.
10. He likes … have fun while you practise.

The bad instructor

1. He has … start on a steep slope.
2. He never explains … walk up a slope.
3. He expects … do movements he hasn't explained properly.
4. He doesn't show … use your knees and hips.
5. He wants … do difficult turns before teaching you the easy ones.
6. He doesn't show … avoid falls.
7. He never tells … get back on your feet again.
8. He makes … do the same things for a whole week.
9. He prefers … practise on your own.
10. He hates … ask questions.

89 Travelling by Pullman

1. *On my first visit to the USA in the late forties, I planned to travel on one of those luxurious Pullman trains which took three nights and two days to cross the continent. Never having had such an experience before, I asked an American friend:*

a) Where should I take my baggage to in the station?
b) Where can I find a porter?
c) What should I take with me to my compartment?
d) How much should I tip the porter?
e) When should I tip the steward?
f) How can I regulate the temperature of my compartment?
g) Where can I get some refreshments during the journey?
h) When should I go for dinner?
i) How can I reserve a seat in the diner?
j) How can I change the seat into a bed?

My friend was very helpful. He explained to me ...
a) where to take my baggage to in the station.
Go on. Use question words + infinitives.

2. My friend gave me some special advice on how to get the best service from the steward, e.g. Hand the steward a tip (expect).
The steward will **expect you to hand** him a tip.
He can regulate the air-conditioning (ask).
Ask him how to regulate the air-conditioning.

a) He will change your seat into a bed (have).
b) Don't wait too long with your tip (I warn).
c) Give him five dollars (advise).
d) He will take your baggage to your compartment (tell).
e) He can put away your heavy baggage (have).
f) He can decide when you should go for dinner (let).
g) He will serve you some refreshments at bedtime (ask).
h) Tell him to wake you in time for breakfast (Tell him you want).
i) Don't miss the excellent breakfast they serve on the train (I'd hate).
j) He will want to talk to you about his problems (let).

90 Joan's Party

1. *Fill in suitable objects (e.g. Joan, her parents, brothers, sisters) and an infinitive with or without* to.

   a) Mr and Mrs Webster allowed ... (invite) a great number of friends to a party.
   b) They let ... (have) the whole of the ground floor.
   c) Joan, who was always giving orders to everyone, expected ... (buy) the drinks.
   d) What's more, she got ... (purchase) an expensive new record-player.
   e) Then she had ... (move) all the furniture out of the dining-room.
   f) Next she made ... (put up decorations) in all the rooms.
   g) She wanted ... (make) a whole mountain of sandwiches.
   h) She asked ... (stay) in their room during the party.
   i) Her parents warned ... (drink) too much.

2. *Read the completed sentences once more. List all those verbal structures that can be translated by German "lassen" ("veran-/zulassen").*

3. **To have**

   a) jdn. veranlassen etwas zu tun

She	had	them	prepare	everything.
	Verb	**Object**	**Infinitive** (cf. RP, p. 94, 2a)	

   b) etwas veranlassen, machen lassen

She	had	everything	prepared.
	Verb	**Object**	**Past Participle** (passive)

   Note the word order in: She *had prepared* everything. (Past Perfect)

4. **Translation**

   a) Am nächsten Morgen ließ Joan niemanden länger als bis 7.30 Uhr schlafen.
   b) Zuerst ließ sie ihre Brüder die Möbel wieder in das Eßzimmer schaffen.
   c) Danach ließ sie ihren Freund die Dekorationen abnehmen.
   d) Sie brachte sogar Jenny dazu (get), die Böden zu putzen.
   e) Als nächstes ließ sie einen ihrer Gäste, einen jungen Ingenieur, kommen, da der Plattenspieler kaputt war.
   f) Sie wollte nicht, daß ihr Vater den Schaden entdeckte.
   g) Dann ließ sie die Aschenbecher leeren, das Geschirr waschen und die Flaschen in den Keller bringen.
   h) Nachdem Joan alles wieder an seinen Platz hatte stellen lassen, bemerkte sie zufrieden: „Wenn wir auf diese Weise zusammenarbeiten, werden uns unsere Eltern sicher wieder eine Party feiern lassen." (have a party)

B ing-Forms Introducing Adverbial and Defining Phrases

91 Refresher Patterns

ing-forms introducing adverbial and defining phrases are usually preferred in formal (written, literary) English as a means of syntactic compression.

1. a) At the beginning of her first riding-lesson Mrs Davidson encouraged her horse **by pulling** *at the reins.*	ing-form introducing an adverbial phrase a) with certain prepositions (gerund)
b) **Although smiling,** she was really very frightened and held on tight.	b) with conjunctions, to make the meaning clear (participle)
c) **Feeling** *the pressure*, the horse broke into a gallop and threw her out of the saddle.	c) without conjunctions (several meanings are possible: as .../ when ... (participle)
2. Some small boys **sitting** *on a nearby fence* roared with laughter.	ing-form introducing a defining phrase (participle)

Note: Da sie immer nervöser wurde, wollte sie nicht an das Pferd herangehen.
Getting more and more nervous, she refused to go near the horse.
Da das Pferd immer nervöser wurde, wollte sie sich ihm nicht nähern.
With the horse getting more and more nervous, she refused to go near it.
subject subject
When used with *with* this structure always demands a subject of its own (in the object case).

"You're not helping your case
by addressing me as 'Madam Chairman'!"

92 A Busy Man

Rewrite the following sentences; use versions containing ing-forms as a means of syntactic compression.

1. The Secretary of State plans to visit all those countries which export oil to the USA.
2. As he takes their good will for granted, he will offer them a fair deal.
3. He will suggest prices that correspond to last year's standards.
4. Since he believes that both sides are interested in a quick solution, he is quite optimistic.
5. As the US Administration is in favour of free trade, he will reject all export restrictions.
6. After he has left the Middle East he will go to London.
7. Although he generally disagrees with Britain's oil policy, he will offer technical aid for projects which concern the drilling for North Sea oil.
8. After he has made this offer he expects that Britain will have to agree to US participation in the projects.
9. As such projects demand public money the Administration has a vital interest in a satisfactory agreement.
10. He has the full support of the President in these matters and therefore can pursue all projects with the necessary authority.
11. Before he goes on to Ottawa, where he will attend a conference which is to deal with the pipe-lining of Alaskan oil, he will talk to the British Prime Minister.
12. When he returns to the USA he will be just in time for the annual session of the UN General Assembly.

93 Would You Know What to Do?

1. An instructor of a first-aid course gives the following descriptions of accidents to the members of his class:
   a) Your little girl has been stung on the neck by an insect.
   She comes into the kitchen. She is screaming with pain.
   b) A little boy comes running up to you. He is crying bitterly.
   He has been bitten in the leg by a dog.
   c) Your baby is rolling on the floor and kicking her legs in the air. She is choking violently. A button which is sticking in her windpipe theatens to suffocate her.

d) Your father returns from a long and exhausting car ride. He staggers into the house. He presses his hand against his head and complains of dizziness.

e) Your neighbour is lying injured under his apple-tree. He cannot move his broken leg from under the fallen ladder.

f) Your friend who lives several blocks away calls you on the phone because she feels that something is wrong with her gas-heating. When you reach her home you find her in the kitchen where she is lying unconscious on the floor.

Annotations

to choke to be unable to breathe – **to suffocate** to kill by making breathing impossible – **to stagger** to walk unsteadily – **dizziness** feeling that everything is turning round

2. Two weeks later the course is given a test in which the same accidents are presented to them in *written* form:

a) Having been stung on the neck by an insect, your little girl comes into the kitchen screaming with pain.

Go on. Write a compressed version of text 1 by using ing-forms.

94 A Quiet Little Place in the Country (Translation)

▼ *Translate these extracts from a newspaper article which describes how disappointing life in the country can be. Use ing-forms as part of adverbial and defining phrases where possible.*

1. Da ich dem Lärm und der Unruhe der Stadt entfliehen wollte, kaufte ich ein altes Bauernhaus auf dem Lande.
2. Vor einem Monat zog ich ein und hoffte, dort Ruhe und Frieden zu finden.
3. Am ersten Morgen, als ich am Frühstückstisch saß, hörte ich ein Klopfen an der Tür.
4. Der Bauer, der auf der anderen Seite der Straße wohnte, kam, um mich zu fragen, ob ich ihm einen Spaten leihen könne.
5. Wer hat je von einem Bauern gehört, der sich einen Spaten leihen muß?
6. Da ich den Mann jetzt recht gut kenne, bin ich überzeugt, daß er nur gekommen war, um herauszufinden, ob ich irgendwo eine exotische Geliebte (mistress) versteckt hatte.
7. Während der nächsten paar Stunden erschienen mehrere Dorfbewohner, die sich Zucker, eine Zwiebel oder ein Pfund Mehl leihen wollten.

8. Während ich mit ihnen sprach, wurde mir klar, daß sie lediglich gekommen waren, um nachzusehen, ob ich verheiratet, verrückt, verschuldet oder in Schwierigkeiten war.
9. Als eine alte Frau auf dem Küchentisch eine leere Whiskyflasche entdeckte, nannte sie mich einen Säufer (drunkard).
10. Sobald der Pfarrer davon hörte, kam er in mein Haus gestürzt, um mit mir zu reden.
11. Nachdem mir mein Nachbar am nächsten Morgen zugesehen hatte, wie ich drei Stunden lang im Garten arbeitete, sagte er mir schließlich, daß ich fast alles falsch gemacht hätte.
12. Obwohl ich wußte, wie das Leben in der Stadt ist, gab ich am Ende auf und verkaufte das Haus.

95 Faith and Hope

In Joseph Conrad's novel Lord Jim *800 Moslem pilgrims set out on a pilgrimage from an Indian port.*

They streamed aboard over three gangways, they streamed in urged by faith and the hope of paradise, without a word, a murmur, or a look back. They spread on all sides over the deck, flowed forward and aft, filled the inner recesses of the ship – like water filling a cistern, like water flowing into crevices, like water running silently even with the rim. Eight hundred men and women with faith and hopes, with affections and memories, they had collected there, coming from north and south and from the outskirts of the East, after treading the jungle paths, descending the rivers, crossing in small canoes from island to island, passing through suffering, meeting strange sights, beset by strange fears, upheld by one desire.

They came covered with dust, with sweat, with rags – the strong men at the head of family parties, the lean old men pressing forward without hope of return; young boys with fearless eyes glancing curiously, shy little girls with long hair; the timid women clasping to their breasts, wrapped in loose ends of soiled headcloths, their sleeping babies.

Abridged from *Lord Jim*, by Joseph Conrad.

Annotations

aft to the back – **the inner recesses** [ri'sesiz] the inside – **cistern** ['sistən] tank for storing water – **crevice** ['krevis] narrow opening or crack – **even with the rim** up to the edge – **outskirts** outer regions – **beset** bedrängt – **lean** thin

1. *Translate the text.*
2. *Which German structures did you use to translate the defining or adverbial phrases introduced by ing-forms?*

C ing-Forms After Certain Expressions

96 Refresher Patterns

1. The horse just *stood* **waiting** for some kind of a signal from its rider.	ing-form (participle) after a number of verbs expressing rest or movement; cf. list 1
2. But as Mrs Davidson was afraid of the horse, she *avoided* **pulling** at the reins.	ing-form (gerund) after a number of verbs; cf. list 2
3. "*It's no use* **expecting** the horse to read your thoughts," shouted the instructor.	ing-form (gerund) after phrases like *it's no use, it's useless, what's the use of, it's worth (while)*
4. With the instructor's help Mrs Davidson finally *succeeded in* **making** the horse take a few steps forward.	ing-form (gerund) after a) verbs b) adjectives } + prepositions c) nouns cf. list 3

Note: Many words in lists 2 and 3 may be followed by an ing-form which has a subject of its own (in the object or genitive case):
She insisted on *the instructor('s)* leading the horse.
She insisted on *him* (*his*) leading the horse.
subject subject

1. stand
   sit
   lie
   remain
   come
   go (swimming, shopping, hiking, etc.)

2. avoid
   be busy
   deny
   enjoy
   finish
   give up
   imagine
   keep (on)
   mind
   practise
   suggest

3. a) complain of
   insist on
   look forward to
   object to
   rely on
   succeed in
   talk of/about
   speak of/about

   b) accustomed to
   afraid of
   capable of
   fond of
   interested in
   keen on
   proud of
   tired of
   used to

   c) chance of
   danger of
   difficulty in
   intention of
   opportunity of
   reason for
   way of

1.

"Would you mind holding this nail for me, dear? – I always hit my thumb."

2.

"There was a time, Mildred, when I looked forward to your retiring from show-business."

97 Bird-watching

Donald Swan and Derek Tern are bird-watchers – members of a club whose aim it is to watch, photograph, tape and ring wild birds. The following passage is from Donald's diary written on a bird-watching expedition to the Western Isles of Scotland.

July 21st: Finished weighing the eggs taken from the nests, while Derek kept on ringing fledgeling gulls. Gave up repairing our 16 mm camera. Don't think it worth while spending any more time on the damned thing. Shall have to get used to shooting all films with the 8 mm camera. Bad luck!
July 22nd: Derek insists on taking flashlights for single shots. Doesn't see any danger of disturbing hens sitting on their nests. Up to now most of them remained sitting on their eggs, even with us taking pictures from very close up.
July 23rd: Enjoyed watching fledgelings making first attempts to leave nests, with the hens standing on guard nearby. Practised imitating hens' call and succeeded in attracting a number of fledgelings, which came rushing towards me at the first call.
July 24th: Walking over to the cliffs this morning hit upon nest containing four strangely coloured eggs. Looking at it more closely decided nest must have been deserted for some time. Although having scruples took eggs with me.
July 25th: Derek evidently doesn't mind breaking his neck for a chance of taking some close-up shots of herring gulls nesting on the cliffs. No use objecting to his taking risks. True bird-watchers seem capable of doing almost anything.

Annotations
fledgeling young bird just able to fly – **gull** Möwe – **flashlight** *here:* photo flashlight, device for producing brilliant light

1. *Translate Donald's diary into German.*
2. *List and explain an example for each of the four patterns described in the Refresher Patterns No 96, p. 103.*
3. *Use Donald's notes to write a report for his club magazine. Make use of ing-forms.*
4. *Rewrite the following sentences by using the expressions given in brackets together with an ing-form. Don't change the meaning of the sentences.*
   Example: Think I can trust that Derek will be careful (rely).
   Think I can rely on Derek('s) being careful.

a) Derek very proud because he has ringed his 100th gull (be proud).
b) Doesn't consider it difficult to ring another 100 (see no difficulty).
c) Today big hen dashed at me (come), while I was ringing fledgelings (be busy).
d) So just waited until the hen calmed down (stand).
e) Too bad Derek was having a swim at that moment (go).
f) If we had been able to shoot this scene (succeed), we might have made our film more dramatic (chance).
g) It may be a good idea to go back to that nest another time with the camera (be worth while).
h) On the other hand we shouldn't change camera positions too often (avoid).
i) Derek is angry because we have already used up so much film material (complain).
j) Tried in vain to tell him that our films will make a lot of money (no use).

98 Hitch-hiking

▼ *Form sentences with the following expressions and an ing-form. Complete the sentences in as many different ways as possible.*

1. *Jimmy is keen on travelling but he hasn't much money, so he goes hitchhiking. He says, "I ...*

   a) enjoy
   b) interested
   c) never miss an opportunity
   d) not mind
   e) never give up
   f) chance
   g) succeed
   h) see no reason

2. *Jimmy's sister, Sandra, never goes hitch-hiking. She says, "I ...*

   a) not interested
   b) better ways
   c) object
   d) not enjoy
   e) tired
   f) not accustomed
   g) afraid
   h) dangers

3. *Use some of the expressions from 1 and 2 to say what* you *think about hitch-hiking.*

99 Shooting an Elephant

In the 1920s the English writer George Orwell served in Burma as an officer of the British Imperial Police. One day an elephant went wild and the crowd, who had gathered to watch the scene, expected Orwell to shoot the animal.

They had seen the rifle and were all shouting excitedly that I was going to shoot the elephant. They had not shown much interest in the elephant when he was merely ravaging their homes, but it was different now that he was going to be shot. It was a bit of fun to them, as it would be to an English crowd; besides, they wanted the meat. It made me vaguely uneasy. I had no intention of shooting the elephant – I had merely sent for the rifle to defend myself if necessary – and it is always unnerving to have a crowd following you. I marched down the hill, looking and feeling a fool, with the rifle over my shoulder and an ever-growing army of people jostling at my heels.

The elephant was standing eight yards from the road, his left side towards us. He took not the slightest notice of the crowd's approach. He was tearing up bunches of grass, beating them against his knees to clean them and stuffing them into his mouth.

I had halted on the road. As soon as I saw the elephant I knew with perfect certainty that I ought not to shoot him. It is a serious matter to shoot a working elephant – it is comparable to destroying a huge and costly piece of machinery – and obviously one ought not to do it if it can possibly be avoided. And at that distance, peacefully eating, the elephant looked no more dangerous than a cow.

But then I glanced round. I looked at the sea of yellow faces – faces all happy and excited over this bit of fun, all certain that the elephant was going to be shot. At that moment I knew that I would have to shoot the elephant.

When I pulled the trigger I did not hear the bang or feel the kick, but I heard the devilish roar of glee that went up from the crowd.

Abridged from *Shooting an Elephant*, by George Orwell.

Annotations

to ravage to plunder, ruin – **to jostle** ['dʒɔsl] to push – **comparable** ['kɔmpərəbl] – **trigger** part of a gun pulled with the finger in order to fire it – **glee** feeling of joy

1. *Where in the text are ing-forms used*
   a) *as part of the continuous form;*
   b) *as adjectives?*

2. *Use the words given below to describe Orwell's dilemma:*
   a) try to avoid
   b) see no reason
   c) have no intention ... what the crowd wanted
   d) not be used to ... a hostile crowd
   e) not succeed ... the people
   f) see no way

3. *Use the following words to describe the behaviour of the crowd:*
   a) enjoy
   b) see an opportunity ... fun
   c) look forward ... Orwell
   d) be keen ... the meat
   e) not mind the officer ... a working elephant
   f) give him no chance ... the elephant's life
   g) keep on

D ing-Forms or Infinitive Structures (Mixed Exercises)

100 Refresher Patterns

ing-forms (cf. also RPs p. 99, 103)	**infinitive** (cf. also RP p. 94)
1.a) Professor Myers usually *begins* **lecturing** at 9 o'clock.	Professor Myers usually *begins* **to lecture** at 9 o'clock.
begin, start, continue can take an ing-form or an infinitive	
b) He *likes* **making** jokes wherever possible.	But yesterday he said: "Today I'*d like* **to talk** about a very serious problem."
After *hate, like, love, prefer*	
the ing-form expresses a general statement or describes a habit	the infinitive is preferred when the speaker refers to a particular situation *(today)*, especially with *would* and *should*
c) He *stopped* **talking** when a student wanted to ask him a question.	He *stopped* **to answer** the student's question.
After *stop, go on*	
the ing-form expresses an action which has been going on and is now brought to an end, or continued	the infinitive expresses purpose (cf. *in order to* answer); it refers to a new action
d) Then another student said he *remembered* **reading (having read)** his theory in Professor Maxwell's latest book.	Professor Myers said that he had *forgotten* **to mention** his source.
After *remember, forget* or *regret*	
the ing-form expresses that s.th. has taken place	the infinitive expresses that s.th. is/was still to take place.
2. When he *saw* some students **laughing** he became rather angry.	The students *heard* him **say:** "Stupid fools."
ing-form after verbs of perception: the action is in progress	infinitive without *to* after verbs of perception: the action is complete

Note: Teaching (To teach) is one of the duties of a university professor.
The ing-form or the infinitive may be used for the subject of a sentence.

1.

"For heaven's sake turn over Tom and stop breathing down my neck like a horse!"

2.

"But I only stopped to tell you I'd passed my driving test, Dad."

101 The Speculator

Put in ing-forms or infinitives. Give both versions where possible.

1. (dream) of sudden wealth is my friend Peter's favourite pastime.
2. I think he began (speculate) about a "miracle" when he was still at school and went on (make) plans for its fulfilment throughout his life.
3. I remember (meet) him once when he had just bought a piece of absolutely useless land, because he had observed several men (walk) up and down the field and (search) the ground.
4. He didn't even stop (ask) them what they were doing; on the contrary he preferred (dash) to the surprised owner and (buy) the land on the spot.
5. Later the owner told me that all the men were doing was (look) for a lost model aeroplane.
6. (worry) about details has never been Peter's way of going about things. His motto is: "I hate (wait) for good luck – you've got to go out and get it!"
7. Once I found him (pile up) flower pots in his garage. He had heard someone (say) that peppermint contained a substance to dissolve gall stones and was going to grow the miracle plant on his terrace.
8. It was not until he started (work) on another promising project that he stopped (grow) peppermint.
9. The true miracle about Peter, however, is this: He never regrets (have spent) time, money, and energy on what – in every single case – he likes (call) his "one and only chance".

102 The Amateur Builder

Put in ing-forms or infinitives.

1. Terry Morgan is a do-it-yourself enthusiast. He enjoys (make) furniture and (do) repairs in the house.
2. These days, however, he is no longer satisfied with (do) mere repair-work; he prefers (knock down) walls or (put in) new windows.
3. His family, therefore, is not surprised when he suggests (instal) a new bathroom or (enlarge) the living-room.
4. Terry never minds (sacrifice) his holidays for enterprises of this sort.
5. Once he has started he hates (be interrupted).
6. With untiring energy he keeps (work) from early in the morning till late at night and doesn't stop (take) a rest.
7. His wife and children are used to (have) their meals without the head of the family, although they can always hear him (saw) or (hammer) somewhere in the house.
8. When he has finished (modernize) a room, he hardly ever remembers (clean up) the mess he has left behind.
9. Mrs Morgan has long since stopped (complain). She carefully avoids (talk) about repairs and improvements so that Terry won't be carried away by any more brilliant ideas.
10. She would love (live) in a home where she doesn't have to step over bricks lying about on floors, but she knows that her husband will probably go on (remodel) their home for the rest of his life.

103 The Shrike and the Chipmunks

Once upon a time there were two chipmunks, a male and a female. The male chipmunk thought that arranging nuts in artistic patterns was more fun than just piling them up to see how many you could pile up. The female was all for piling up as many as you could. She told her husband that if he gave up making designs with the nuts there would be room in their large cave for a great many more and he would soon become the wealthiest chipmunk in the woods. But he would not let her interfere with his designs, so she flew into a rage and left him. "The shrike will get you," she said, "because you are helpless and cannot look after yourself."

The next day the shrike began hanging around outside the chipmunk's cave, waiting to catch him. The shrike couldn't get in because the doorway was blocked with soiled laundry and dirty dishes. "He will come out for a walk after breakfast and I will get him then," thought the shrike. But the chipmunk slept all day and did not get up and have breakfast until after dark. Then he came out for a breath of air before beginning work on a new design. The shrike swooped down to snatch up the chipmunk, but could not see very well on account of the dark, so he batted his head against an alder branch and was killed.

A few days later the female chipmunk returned and saw the awful mess the house was in. She went to the bed and shook her husband. "What would you do without me?" she demanded. "Just go on living, I guess," he said. "You wouldn't last five days," she told him. She swept the house and did the dishes and sent out the laundry, and then she made the chipmunk get up and wash and dress. "You can't be healthy if you lie in bed all day and never get any exercise," she told him. So she took him for a walk in the bright sunlight and they were both caught and killed by the shrike's brother, a shrike named Stoop.

Moral: Early to rise and early to bed makes a male healthy and wealthy and dead.

Annotations

shrike kind of bird, also called "butcher-bird" (Würger) – **chipmunk** squirrel-like animal (Backenhörnchen) – **to interfere with** to disturb, interrupt – **soiled laundry** *here:* dirty clothes – **to swoop down** to come down with a rush – **to snatch** to seize, grasp – **alder** ['ɔ:ldə] Erle

1. *Say what the female chipmunk*
   a) expected her husband to do;
   b) did not want him to do;
   c) finally made him do.

2. *Say what the male chipmunk*
   a) did not want to do;
   b) caused his wife to do;
   c) did not let her do.

3. *To answer the following questions use ing-forms.*
   a) What was the male chipmunk fond of doing?
   b) What did the female chipmunk think made life worth living?
   c) What did she think her husband incapable of doing after she had left him?
   d) What, obviously, gave her great satisfaction after her return?
   e) What killed him finally?

104 Gwendolyn and Her Father

Have Sir Archibald and Gwendolyn each tell the story from their point of view:

1.

a) *Sir Archibald:*

b) *Gwendolyn:*

2.

a) be busy/write
hear/serenade

b) sit/sew
hear/fill the air

3.

a) hate/be disturbed
jump up/go

b) stop/sew
go/run

4.

a) look out/notice/
stand

b) notice/look up
stop/play
start/shake all over

5.

a) see/leap headfirst
over the wall

b) watch/jump over the
wall

6.

a) return/continue

b) fetch a mirror/
examine my face/
wonder

105 Will Power Versus Horse Power (Translation)

1. Anfangs September bemerkte ich, daß zwei deutsche Studenten in Mrs Wrigleys Mansarden (attic) einzogen.
2. Gegen Ende des Monats begannen sie, kleine Gelegenheitsarbeiten für ihre amerikanischen Nachbarn zu übernehmen (do little odd jobs).
3. Wir beobachteten, wie sie Gehwege fegten, Wagen wuschen und Laub zusammenharkten (rake up).
4. Ich erinnerte mich, daß ich Mrs Wrigley sagen hörte, daß nach Mexico zu fahren, der große Traum der beiden Jungen sei.
5. Es war anfangs Dezember, als ich sie unter, in und aus einem 1949er Ford kriechen sah.
6. Diesmal hielt ich an, um mit ihnen zu sprechen.
7. Ich hasse es normalerweise, anderen Leuten zu sagen, was sie zu tun haben, aber diesmal mußte ich es: ihre Kiste (jalopy [dʒə'lɔpi]) war in einem derart schlechten Zustand, daß es mir unverantwortlich schien, sie fahren zu lassen.
8. Während ich mit ihnen sprach, hörten sie nie auf, am Wagen zu arbeiten und ich fand bald heraus, daß es nutzlos war, sie zu warnen.
9. Offensichtlich zogen sie es vor, in Ruhe gelassen zu werden.
10. Ich bedauerte, jemals meine Bedenken erwähnt zu haben, als im Februar – und Wochen nach ihrer Rückkehr von einer 7000-Meilen-Reise nach Mexico – ihre „Kiste“ meinen neuen Cadillac aus einer Schneewächte (snow drift) zog.

106 Playing Tricks with the Telly

In Alan Sillitoe's The Loneliness of the Long-distance Runner *the narrator, a young thief, describes the effects of TV adverts and films on his family:*

And the telly made all these things seem twenty times better than we'd ever thought they were. They were moving around loose, half open packets and tins making you think that all you had to do was finish opening them before they were yours, like seeing an open safe through a shop window with the man gone away for a cup of tea without thinking to guard his money.

The films they showed were good as well, in that way, because we couldn't take our eyes from the cops chasing the robbers who had bags full of money and looked like getting away to spend it – until the last moment. I always hoped they would get away, and could never stop wanting to put my hand out, smash into the screen and get the copper in a half-nelson so's he'd stop following the bloke with the money-bags.

And it was when these cops were chasing the crooks that we played some good tricks with the telly, because when one of them opened his big mouth to talk about getting their man I'd turn the sound down and see his mouth move like a goldfish – it was so funny the whole family nearly split their sides on the new carpet.

It was the best of all though when we did it to some Conservative telling us about how good his government was going to be if we kept on voting for them – their big mouths rolling and opening, so that you could see they didn't mean a word they said, especially with not a word coming out because we'd cut off the sound.

From *The Loneliness of the Long-distance Runner*, by Alan Sillitoe. © Alan Sillitoe, 1960

Annotations

cop, copper (sl.) policeman – **half-nelson** (Ringer-)Griff – **so's he'd stop (so as he would stop)** so that he would stop – **bloke** (sl.) man – **crook** (coll.) dishonest person, criminal – **to split one's sides** to laugh violently

1. *Explain the use of the following ing-forms (cf. RPs p. 94, p. 99, p. 103, p. 108):*
   a) half open packets and tins *making* you think
   b) all you had to do was finish *opening* them
   c) without *thinking* to guard his money
   d) the cops *chasing* the robbers
   e) I could never stop *wanting* to put my hand out
   f) one of them opened his big mouth to talk about *getting* their man
   g) if we kept on *voting* for them
   h) with not a word *coming* out

2. *Explain the use of the following infinitives (cf. RPs p. 94, p. 108):*
   a) And the telly made all these things *seem* twenty times better
   b) I'd see his mouth *move* like a goldfish.

3. *Study the following paraphrase of the original text, lines 2 to 5:*
   Half open packets and tins were moving around loose. They made you think that all you had to do was finish opening them, and then they were yours. It was as if you saw an open safe through a shop window, and as if the man had gone away for a cup of tea without thinking to guard his money.
   Compare the original with the paraphrase and say which version achieves greater clarity. Give reasons.

▼ 4. *Write your own paraphrase of lines 17 to 21 in the same style as 3.*

Articles

A The Definite Article

107 Refresher Patterns

The **definite article** is not used	The **definite article** is used
1. a) **Students** nowadays are often criticized by the older generation.	b) Many old people dislike **the students** *who protest against established traditions.*
before plural nouns in a general sense	before plural nouns, if they are more closely defined (e.g. by a defining relative clause or an of-genitive)
2. a) Young people are generally suspicious of **authority.**	b) Yet they are often willing to accept **the authority** *of someone whom they can trust.*
before abstract nouns used in a general sense	before abstract nouns, if they are more closely defined (cf. Note)
3. a) They show a keen interest in **society** and **man**'s problems in general.	b) They often criticize **the society** *they live in.*
before collective nouns (no plural "s"): *people, society, mankind, man* (der Mensch), *woman* (die Frau)	before collective nouns, if they are more closely defined
4. a) Many of them feel that going to **university** should be more than just receiving an academic training.	b) In some countries **the university** with its halls and lecture-rooms provides a suitable meeting-place for politically-minded students.
with nouns like *university, school, prison, church, hospital,* when their function is referred to	with nouns like *university*, etc. when the building itself or the institution is referred to

Note: The article is not used when adjectives form a unit together with abstract nouns and when the whole term has a general meaning (e.g. *human nature, public opinion, modern history, English literature*).

1.

"I don't know whose dog it is, but I wish people would feed their own animals."

2.

"You *must* cut the lawn – what will the people on the ground floor think?"

108 Sad to Report

In 1974 the government of Sri Lanka (formerly Ceylon) banned all opposition meetings and demonstrations. It also shut down the only independent newspaper group. Some time later, the state-controlled *Ceylon Daily News* carried the following death notice:

> The death occurred under tragic circumstances of
>
> D.E.M. O'Cracy
>
> beloved husband of T. Ruth, loving father of
>
> L.I. Bertie, brother of Faith, Hope and Justitia

Annotations
Ceylon [si'lɔn] – **Justitia** [dʒʌ'stiʃjə]

1. *Read the text of the death notice making clear the original words hidden in the proper names.*
2. *Explain why the definite article cannot be used before the words reconstructed from the proper names (cf. RP, p. 115).*

109 Mankind and Science

1. *Put in the definite article where necessary.*

It is fashionable to criticize the changes that have resulted from ... exploitation of ... science and to express dissatisfaction with the quality of ... life they have produced. Yet an examination of the average condition of ... people, even in the parts of the world where ... human suffering is greatest, makes it clear that the discoveries of both physical and biological science have improved the condition of ... mankind and are continuing to do so.

We do well to recognize clearly the problems of ... overpopulation and ... pollution. But it would be hard to deny that at least for those of us in western countries the quality of ... life has in general improved over the last century. Perhaps those who complain do not realize what their grandfathers suffered from ... poverty, ... ignorance and ... disease.

It is dangerous to make forecasts, but it seems unlikely that ... exploitation of ... science will be stopped. There may be a retreat from ... science in some western countries but less developed countries are not impressed by our scruples.

The desire to live and to improve ... life is strongly implanted in ... men. But if ... people are to have a full life they will have to learn as soon as possible to respect ... environment, both physical and biological.

From *The Sunday Times*, London, 17 November, 1974

2. *Compare:* the exploitation of science – die Ausbeutung **der** Naturwissenschaften. *Find more examples from the text where the English expression does not have a definite article whereas the German translation does.*

110 Youth and Society

1. *Put in the definite article where necessary.*

... youth of today no longer accepts the given standards of ... society. Many young people are not satisfied with ... life they are forced to lead: they leave ... home, often before they have finished ... school or refuse to seek ... security of a job. ... adults look for reasons for this dropping out of ... society. Is ... younger generation afraid to accept ... responsibility? Or are they too lazy to work and do they just want to enjoy ... life? With some this may be true, but with many it is an act of ... protest, a form of ... rebellion. They reject a materialistic outlook on ... life and refuse to take up the role of consumers in ... interests of ... big business. ... productivity and ... economic growth have become something to be distrusted; ... technology, in their opinion, has advanced so far that it now threatens to destroy ... nature, ... ecological balance in the world and eventually ... mankind itself. They feel that ... man must love his fellow man instead of constantly competing in the name of .... profit and ... progress. ... competitive society of today with its traditional values fails to show them a purpose in ... life.

Annotations
to compete [kəm'pi:t] to try to get ahead of others – **competitive society** [kəm'petitiv] Leistungsgesellschaft

▼ 2. *Use the nouns in italics to form a sentence of your own in which the new context demands the definite article for the noun; e.g.*
Young people often want to change *society.*
The *society* they want to establish is one free from competition and stress.

a) *Young people* are as a rule critical of the older generation.
b) They find *life* dull and uninteresting.
c) *Security* is not of great importance to many young people.
d) To their parents *jobs* are a guarantee of security.
e) *Responsibility* is not always readily accepted by the young.
f) Big business leads, in the opinion of young people, to *materialism.*
g) In their opinion *economic growth* is not a desirable end in itself.
h) They don't believe in *technology* as the only means of human progress.
i) For them *progress* means an improvement in man's behaviour.
j) From the point of view of the younger generation *traditional values* have failed.

111 **Theory and Experience** (Translation)

▼ 1. Warren Clifford und ich wurden Freunde in den dreißiger Jahren während unseres ersten Semesters an der Universität.
2. Warren war besonders interessiert an Themen wie dem technischen Fortschritt und seinen Auswirkungen auf die Gesellschaft.
3. Sein Motto war: „Die Zeiten haben sich gewandelt, und der Mensch muß sich mit ihnen wandeln."
4. Und er fügte hinzu, daß nach seiner Meinung das Transportwesen (transportation) das Leben des modernen Menschen bestimmen (shape) werde.
5. Das mag der Grund gewesen sein, weshalb er beschloß, die Herausforderung der Technologie anzunehmen, indem er sich für ungefähr 50 Pfund einen klapprigen (rickety) alten Morris kaufte.

6. Damals durften die Studenten keinen Wagen haben, und deshalb mußte er ihn immer in einiger Entfernung von der Universität parken.
7. Die Erfahrung, die Warren mit dem Morris machte (have), war kurz und dramatisch: nach mehreren Pannen – die meisten[1] davon in dichtem Verkehr – ließ er sein Auto in der Straße, wo er es gewöhnlich parkte, stehen.
8. Warren hatte allen Glauben an den Fortschritt und natürlich auch an den Menschen, der ihm den Wagen verkauft hatte, verloren.
9. Sein Glaube an die Gerechtigkeit und die Menschheit wurde jedoch rasch wiederhergestellt (restore), als eine ältere Dame auf den geparkten Morris auffuhr (drive into) und ihre Versicherung ihm 60 Pfund zahlte.

[1] *most of them, most students, both friends* etc. without the definite article.

B The Indefinite Article

112 Refresher Patterns

1. Jack Donald is **a Scotsman.** 2. He was **a university professor** before he became **a politician.** 3. He is **a Conservative** and **a Protestant.** 4. He is regarded *as* **an expert** in sociology.	In 1971 Jack Donald held the office of **vice-president,** two years later he was appointed **president** of the college.
The **indefinite article** is used before nouns denoting 1. nationality, 2. a profession, 3. membership or religion, 4. after *as.*	The **indefinite article** is not used when a title or an office can only be held by one person at a time.

"Actually, madam, I'm a Doctor of *Philosophy*!"

113 Family Tradition

A Conservative was once addressing an audience during an election campaign. "Is there by any chance a Socialist in the house?" he asked.
"Yes, here!" shouted a voice from the back. "I'm a Socialist."
"Would you mind telling the audience why you're a Socialist?"
"Well," he said, "my grandfather was a Socialist, my father was a Socialist, and so I'm a Socialist."
"That means if your grandfather had been a swindler and your father had been a swindler, you'd be a swindler, too, Sir?"
"Certainly not," he replied, "I'd be a Conservative."

1. *Where in the text is the indefinite article used as described in the Refresher Patterns? Explain why.*
2. *Retell the anecdote.*

114 Sir Winston Churchill (1874–1965)

1. *Dates from the life of Sir Winston Churchill:*
   1894 officer in the British army
   1898 war correspondent in the Boer War
   1900 Member of Parliament for Oldham (Conservative)
   1906 Liberal Member of Parliament
   1911 First Lord of the Admiralty
   1915 war volunteer
   1917 War Secretary
   1924 Conservative again; Chancellor of the Exchequer
   1940 Prime Minister
   1945 Leader of the Opposition
   1951 Prime Minister
   1955 Government backbencher

2. *Form sentences to describe Churchill's career. Use the following verbs and phrases:*

be made	become
be given the office/position of	be appointed/re-appointed
serve as	be elected/re-elected
work as	

115 **Billy the Kid and Pat Garret** (Translation)

▼ 1. Als Billy the Kid 17 Jahre alt war, arbeitete er als Cowboy auf John H. Turnstalls Ranch.
2. Turnstall war Engländer. Er hatte sich in Lincoln County, New Mexico, niedergelassen, wo er Viehzüchter (cattle-breeder) geworden war.
3. Billy wurde als freundlicher und hilfsbereiter Junge geschildert, aber er war schon als Revolverheld (gun-fighter) bekannt.
4. Als sein Boss, den Billy als wahren Freund betrachtete, erschossen wurde, beschloß er, die Mörder zu töten.
5. Einige berüchtigte (notorious) Revolverhelden schlossen sich ihm an, und Billy wurde zum Führer der Bande gemacht. Bald wurde der Cowboy zum Killer.
6. 1880 versprach ein Mann aus Alabama, Pat Garret, Gesetz und Ordnung wiederherzustellen, und die Leute von Lincoln County wählten ihn zum Sheriff.
7. Pat Garret hielt sein Versprechen auf seine Weise: er erschoß Billy, ohne ihm eine Chance zu geben, seinen Revolver zu ziehen.
8. Billy wurde eine berühmte Figur im Westen. Der Posten eines Sheriffs von Lincoln County wurde jedoch einem andern Mann übergeben, weil die Leute in Garret einen feigen Mörder sahen.
9. Fünf Jahre später ernannte ihn der Gouverneur von Texas zum Kapitän der Texas Rangers, aber nach ein paar Monaten mußte Garret auch diesen Posten aufgeben.
10. 1901 bekam er eine letzte Chance: er wurde Zollinspektor in El Paso. 4 Jahre später wurde er auf dem Weg zu seiner Ranch getötet. Der Mörder wurde freigesprochen (acquit).

Indefinite Adjectives and Pronouns

A Some – Any

116 Refresher Patterns

some (-body, -one, -thing) is used to express that something actually exists	**any** (-body, -one, -thing) is used to express that something does not exist or that its existence is uncertain
1. a) I'll get **some** wood to make a fire.	There isn't **any** wood around here.
in **affirmative statements**	in **negative statements**
b) We shouldn't go back *without* at least **some** wood to start a fire with.	There are *hardly* **any** trees to be seen.
after *without* if the **meaning** of the statement is **affirmative**	after *without* and *hardly (scarcely)* if the **meaning** of the statement is **negative**
2. a) Could you give me **some** matches, please? b) Shall I give you **some** paper handkerchiefs? c) Couldn't we use **some** dry grass?	Have we got **any** paper to start the fire with?
in **questions** expressing a) a request b) an offer c) a suggestion } when a positive answer is expected	in **questions** when it is uncertain what the answer will be
3. a) If only we had **some** newspapers to start the fire with! b) If we took **some** petrol from the car, we might get the fire going.	If you had **any** sense at all you wouldn't have chosen this place for a picnic.
in **if-clauses** expressing a) a wish; b) that the condition (or suggestion) may be fulfilled	in **if-clauses** when the speaker believes that the condition cannot be fulfilled

1.

"Let's have some kids of our own, then invite *them* over."

2.

117 Picnickers

Brenda and Joyce are picnicking with a group of young people. They have been sent away to find some dry wood for a fire. Put in some *or* any.

Brenda: Let's get … dry grass for the fire.
Joyce: There isn't … dry grass after this afternoon's rainfall.
Brenda: Should we break … twigs from those bushes over there? If there's … wood around here at all, it must be there.
Joyce: There aren't … dry twigs on green bushes. We took … green twigs last time and they wouldn't burn.
Brenda: Maybe … of the others have found … wood in the meantime.
Joyce: By the way, have you got … idea where we are? Have you seen … of the others around?
Brenda: If … of them were nearby, we'd be able to hear them.
Joyce: Are you sure we'll find the way back without … difficulty? There's hardly …. light now and I'm getting scared.
Brenda: … of the boys should have come with us.
Joyce: They went back to Ashby to get … more coke and beer. I'm sure … of them would have preferred to come along with us, though.
Brenda: I can't think of … who would have refused.
Joyce: I'd be only too glad if … of them were here now.

118 **Stranded** (Translation)

For the following translation keep in mind that English often makes use of not ... any/anything/anyone/anybody/anywhere *instead of* no/nothing/no one/nobody/nowhere, *e.g.* There isn't any water here. *instead of:* There is no water here.

At Dover the luggage of a visiting German youth group was put on the bus of a Dutch group by mistake.

1. Wir fanden niemanden, der uns helfen konnte.
2. Die Polizei sagte, sie (they) könne nichts für uns tun.
3. „Euer Gepäck wird sicherlich irgendwo auftauchen", sagte ein Polizist.
4. „Irgend jemand wird es schließlich finden", fügte ein anderer Bobby hinzu.
5. Sie hatten keine Ahnung, wohin der holländische Bus gefahren war.
6. Wir kannten niemanden.
7. Wir hatten kein Geld.
8. Wir konnten nichts zu essen kaufen.
9. Wir konnten keine Telefongespräche führen.
10. Wir konnten nirgendwo ein Hotel finden.
11. Es gab auch keine Gelegenheit, so spät von Dover wegzukommen.
12. Es schien im Moment keine Hoffnung zu geben, daß wir unser Gepäck wiedersehen würden.
13. Um 23 Uhr kam ein Mann an, der mit der holländischen Gruppe irgendwo in der Nähe von Canterbury gesprochen hatte.
14. Er hatte sogar jemand rufen hören: „Irgend jemand muß das Gepäck der Gruppe verwechselt haben."

119 **Mysterious**

Use some (-body/-one, -thing), any (-body/-one, -thing) *to complete the text*;

e.g. So you, too, heard ... calling upstairs?	So you, too, heard **somebody** calling upstairs?
I wonder if	I wonder if there's **anything** wrong up there.

On a hiking tour across a very lonely part of Northumberland Eric and Carol come to a mysterious-looking old farm house. They start to explore it:

1. *Eric:* There doesn't seem to be ... around.
   Hallo! Is ..... ?
2. *Carol:* If ... were in the house at all, they would have heard you.
   Although, when we came up the drive-way I .....

3. *Eric:* I couldn't see ... anywhere.
I wonder .....

4. *Carol:* Listen! I think I just heard .... .
Look! A cow! So .....

5. *Eric:* There aren't ... windows open on this side.
Let's go round to the other side .....

6. *Carol:* Look! That window hasn't got ... panes.
The broken pieces are still on the window-sill. It looks as if .... .

7. *Eric:* Here are ... fresh footprints on the ground.
Surely .....

8. *Carol:* Can you see ... inside?
What's the matter? You look so pale. .....?

9. *Eric:* Oh God! ... terrible must have happened.
Can you see that body under the table? I think .....

10. *Carol:* I knew that ... was wrong here.
Quick, let's .....

11. *Eric:* But where? There isn't ... other farm nearby.
We must go back to the main road and see .....

120 Asparagus and Champagne

Although almost penniless, W. Somerset Maugham once had to invite one of his female admirers to an expensive Paris restaurant for lunch:

She reassured me.
"I never eat anything for luncheon. Just a bite. I couldn't possibly eat anything more unless they had some of those giant asparagus. I should be sorry to leave Paris without having some of them."
My heart sank. I had seen them in the shops, and I knew that they were horribly expensive. My mouth had often watered at the sight of them.
"Madame wants to know if you have any of those giant asparagus," I asked the waiter.
I tried with all my might to will him to say no. A happy smile spread over his broad, priest-like face, and he assured me that they had some so large, so splendid, so tender, that it was a marvel.
"I'm not in the least hungry," my guest sighed, "but if you insist I don't mind having some[1] asparagus."

[1] Although in its form *I don't mind* is a negation, the meaning of the sentence is affirmative: she actually wants to have some asparagus.

I ordered them.

"Aren't you going to have any?" she inquired.

"No, I never eat asparagus."

Then came the question of drink.

"I never drink anything for luncheon," she said.

"Neither do I," I answered promptly.

"Except white wine," she proceeded as though I had not spoken.

"What would you like?" I asked.

She gave me a bright and amicable flash of her white teeth.

"My doctor won't let me drink anything but champagne."

Later, when we walked out of the restaurant, I had the whole month before me and not a penny in my pocket.

Annotations

asparagus [əs'pærəgəs] Spargel – **champagne** [ʃæm'pein] – **luncheon** (formal) lunch – **giant** very big – **to will** to influence s.o. through one's will – **marvel** miracle – **to proceed** to continue – **amicable** ['æmikəbl] friendly – **to give a flash of one's teeth** to show one's sparkling teeth for a short moment

1. *Explain the use of* some (-thing) *and* any (-thing) *in the text (cf. RP p. 123).*
2. *Make up similar statements ("I never ... but if they have ..., I'll take a little.");*
   use: caviare ['kæviɑ:]
   salmon ['sæmən]
   frogs' legs
   Red Burgundy ['bə:gəndi]
   banana split
3. *What does Maugham's guest tell us about her eating and drinking habits and her appetite. Use* any (-thing) *and* some *in your answers.*

B Any – Every – Each

121 Refresher Patterns

1. a) Mrs Watts knew that her husband, Captain Watts, would come home **any** day now.	
b) **Anyone** could see how much she was looking forward to his arrival.	**any/anyone/anybody/anything** in affirmative statements: it doesn't matter which, who or what
c) **Anything** which might hold up her preparations made her nervous.	
2. a) **Every** day the children asked her, "Will it be today?"	
b) **Everyone** was getting more and more excited.	**every/everyone/everybody/everything:** all without exception
c) By Friday she had **everything** ready.	
3. **Each** child had a surprise for the Captain. **Each (of them)** kept it a secret.	**each (each of):** individual members of a group or parts of a whole – one by one Therefore often used in the structure: *each of + (pro)noun*

Note: He bought three presents which cost five pounds **each** (each present cost five pounds); **each:** *per piece* ("je", "pro").

"When I said you could come to me with your problems any time, Green, I meant at the office."

"It amazes me how they find their way back each year."

122 Anything Can Happen in Scotland

In Scotland every turn of the road is a surprise. Each village has its own way of life, each castle its own history, each loch its own beauty. And anything can happen to the fascinated tourist – not only at Loch Ness. But the noble products of Scotland's distilleries will quickly dispel anyone's fears of monsters, ghosts and cold feet.

From the brochure of a Scottish travel agency

1. *Explain the use of the indefinite adjectives and pronouns in the text (cf. RP, p. 128).*
2. *Translate the text.*
3. *Write a similar ad for the town or area where you live.*

123 The Joys of Eating Out

Put in any (-thing, -where), every (-one/-body, -thing, -where), *or* each.

Now and then ... housewife gets tired of cooking. Last Sunday morning my wife sighed, "I can't face cooking today. I'd give ... for a meal out."

"All right," I said. "Where shall we go?" "Oh, just ... . It doesn't matter."

We went to The Red Lion, the restaurant ... goes to in our town. The first disappointment was that ... table was occupied. We had to wait twenty minutes to get a seat. Besides, there were only two waiters and ... was shouting at them to come to their table. After another twenty minutes one of the waiters came over to us. We ... ordered a three-course lunch: soup, steak with green peas and ice-cream for dessert.

The soup came pretty promptly and ... seemed all right. During the next forty-five minutes, however, ... around us was served, but we were still waiting. By now we were ready to eat ... . Finally the waiter appeared with two steaks, ... the size of a fifty-pence piece.

We were still staring both at the "fifty-pence pieces" and at ... other when he dropped the dish with the vegetables. There were peas ... .

Some had found a resting-place among the flowers on my wife's hat. Trying to pick them from among some cherry blossoms the waiter managed to pour some gravy over ... of us.

The silence which suddenly filled the room while ... was staring at us was interrupted by the manager's cheerful "... all right, sir?"

124 Tricksters

1. *Put in* each *or* every.

When my friend Kenneth and I were students our parents sent us money ... month. Not ... student got as much as we did. However ... of us spent more than he had and at the end of ... month we regularly ran out of money. So we sometimes used a trick to get some food or drink for nothing. It went something like this: One of us asked in a grocer's shop, "How much are your apples?" "5 pence ..." answered the grocer. "We'll take three ..." When the grocer had given us the apples we told him that we had changed our minds. Would he give ... of us three pears instead. The grocer did so, we took the pears and walked out of the shop. "You haven't paid for the pears yet," shouted the grocer, "that will be 15 pence ..." "But we gave you the apples in their place." "Yes, but you didn't pay for them either." "Of course not," was our reply. "You don't expect us to pay for what we didn't have, do you?" ... time we did this in a shop, the poor victim was so confused that we were out of his shop before he could work out how he had been tricked.

2. *Answer the following questions. Use* every *or* each *in your answers:*
   a) How often did the students' parents send them money?
   b) How much were the apples?
   c) How many apples did each of them take?
   d) How much were they supposed to pay?
   e) What happened whenever they played their trick?

125 Anything Will Do (Translation)

▼ *Use all possible forms for the German "jeder/alles".*

1. Wie Ihnen jeder Psychologe sagen kann, benutzen Kinder fast alles, – Holzstücke, Steine, Muscheln – um damit zu spielen.
2. Jeder dieser Gegenstände stellt das dar, was die Phantasie des Kindes daraus macht.
3. Alles hängt von seiner Fähigkeit ab, jeden Gegenstand mit Leben zu erfüllen.
4. Alles andere – das Material, die Form oder die Anzahl seiner Spielsachen – ist von geringerer Bedeutung.
5. Jede Mutter kann Ihnen sagen, daß jedes Zimmer mehr solcher ‚Spielsachen' enthält, als jeder Erwachsene es sich vorstellen könnte: Schuhe und Tassen, Bücher und Aschenbecher.
6. Und jeder kennt den verärgerten Vater, von dessen Schreibtisch jeder Bleistift, jede Zeitung und jede Pfeife abgeräumt (remove) wurde, um in Menschen, Schnee oder Eisenbahnwagen verwandelt zu werden.
7. In jedem gesunden Kind ist ein natürlicher Drang (urge), Dinge nicht nur anzufassen, sondern auch jedem in seiner Phantasie eine besondere Bedeutung zu geben.
8. Solange jede Gefahr für das Kind ausgeschlossen ist, sollte jeder diesen Vorgang fördern (encourage).

C "sich" (Reflexive and Reciprocal Pronouns)

126 Refresher Patterns

1. After his accident Peter couldn't **move** for several days.	The following English verbs are **not** followed by an equivalent to German "sich": approach — imagine behave (sich verhalten) — move boast — realize change — recover differ from — refuse feel — remember get accustomed to — retire happen
2. In his hospital ward the other patients **introduced themselves** to him.	After a number of verbs the equivalent to German "sich" is the **reflexive pronoun** (*oneself*, etc.)
3. Later he was shown how to **wash and dress (himself).**	Some verbs can be used **with or without** *oneself*, etc. as an equivalent to German "sich": behave (o.s.) (sich gut benehmen) dress (o.s.) — shave (o.s.) hide (o.s.) — wash (o.s.)
4. Naturally all the patients **told each other** how their accidents had happened.	The equivalents to German "sich" in the meaning of "einander" are the **reciprocal pronouns** *each other/one another*

Note: The equivalent to German "sich" is never a personal pronoun (*him*, etc.)

1.

"You must *force* yourself, you poor fellow!"

2.

"– and of course they're such company for each other."

127 An Entirely New Feeling of Distance (Translation)

▼ 1. Viele europäische Touristen können sich nicht vorstellen, daß das Reisen in den USA sich beträchtlich vom Reisen in Europa unterscheidet.
2. Sie erwarten oft, daß sie sich in Amerika bald zu Hause fühlen werden.
3. Solche Ansichten ändern sich schon nach (after only) ein paar Tagen in New York zum Beispiel.
4. Ich erinnere mich, daß wir uns an unserem ersten Tag überredeten, von unserem Hotel in der 32. Straße zu einem Konzert in der 77. Straße zu Fuß zu gehen.
5. Wir kamen dort an, als das Konzert beinahe zu Ende war und begannen, uns gegenseitig wegen unserer Dummheit Vorwürfe zu machen (blame for), sobald wir uns von unserem Sechskilometer-Marsch erholt hatten.
6. Ich schämte mich besonders, da ich einen Stadtplan von Manhattan hatte und mich hartnäckig geweigert hatte, die Entfernung nachzusehen.
7. Zuerst versuchte ich mich zu verteidigen, indem ich erklärte, daß ich Meilen mit Kilometern verwechselt hatte.
8. Für den Rest des Abends sprachen wir nicht [mehr] miteinander.
9. Später zog ich mich in eine stille Bar zurück, wo ich mich mit der Umrechnung von (conversion of … into) Kilometern in Meilen beschäftigte.
10. Ich brauchte genau sieben *bourbons*, um mich an ein völlig neues Gefühl für Entfernungen zu gewöhnen.

128 Fifteen Years Later

Complete the following text.

1. When we left school in 1962 we (not realize) how much each of us would (change) within a few years.
2. There was Joe Cowle, for instance. As a schoolboy he always looked as if (never wash). Besides, more than anything else he (enjoy) provoking his teachers.
3. I (remember) that our class (get accustomed to) his being caned at least once a week.
4. Naturally, when, fifteen years later, a class reunion took place, I (imagine) that Joe would still (behave) in the same way.
5. Not until he (introduce) did I recognize him in the quiet, well-mannered gentleman, who – almost shyly – (approach) the table at which I was sitting with some old friends.

6. Most of us had (hug) when we met, but with Joe you got the impression that he (feel) embarrassed about any kind of intimacy.
7. All evening, while most of us (boast) about the tricks we had played on our teachers, Joe didn't seem (be enjoying).
8. He simply (refuse) to laugh at anything, and it wasn't until we (say good-bye to) that I learned that Joe had become the headmaster of the strictest boarding school in the country.

129 Unhappy Ending

Janet tells a friend the story of her romance with Bob from her point of view. Use the following verbs and phrases with reflexive or reciprocal pronouns if possible.

1. *Last year in May*
   meet – introduce –
   fall in love – enjoy
2. *During the first months of our friendship*
   take an interest in – never disagree with –
   trust – be unable to imagine
3. *Gradually*
   change – feel neglected –
   start to argue with – move apart
4. *Then, one evening at a party*
   happen – boast –
   behave like a child –
   refuse to listen – be angry –
   shout at – defend –
   accuse – not speak
5. *From then on*
   fight – annoy –
   reproach – mistrust
6. *Finally*
   behave – care about –
   think of – hate
7. *In the end*
   decide – not see

Adjectives and Adverbs

A Function of Adjectives and Adverbs

130 Refresher Patterns

Adjectives (attributive use)	**Adjectives** (predicative use)	**Adverbs**
1. The **elegant** *schooner* moved out of the bay.	2. In full sail the schooner *looked* **elegant.**	3. a) The schooner *moved* **elegantly** out of the bay. b) On the open sea the wind was **really** *stiff.* c) The boat took the waves **extremely** *well.* d) **Unfortunately** *the weather changed.*
adjectives used attributively qualify nouns	adjectives used predicatively qualify the subject after the following verbs expressing *a state:* be, remain, keep, seem, look, appear *a change of state:* become, grow, get, turn *a perception:* feel, smell, taste, sound	adverbs modify a) verbs b) adjectives c) adverbs d) sentences

1.

"I distinctly told you – *next* Saturday!"

2.

"Hurry up, Chef – the guest at table six is getting impatient!"

131 Fighting Habits With Logic

Jerome stopped fairly regularly at a local pub after work and very often spent the whole evening there. His wife felt extremely annoyed and worried but Jerome seemed absolutely unreasonable and stubbornly refused to listen to her complaints.

So, she wisely changed her tactics. One night she secretly set the alarm clock for 3.00 a.m. The alarm rang and Jerome tiredly got out of bed. When he saw the time he became quite furious. He shouted angrily at his wife and demanded an explanation.

"Well," she replied sweetly, "if it normally takes you five hours to get home from work, I just thought it would also take you five hours to get back to work. And I certainly don't want you to be late."

1. *Make lists of*
   a) all adverbs in the second paragraph (ll. 5–8) which modify verbs;
   b) all adverbs which modify adjectives;
   c) all adverbs which modify adverbs.
2. *Which adjectives in the text are used predicatively*?
3. *Answer the following questions using adverbs where possible.*
   a) What was Jerome's questionable habit?
   b) How did he react to his wife's complaints?
   c) What was his reaction when the alarm rang at 3.00 a.m.?
   d) What was his wife's explanation?

132 Midnight Panic

1. *Read the following introduction to a mystery story and put in the correct forms – adjective or adverb.*

When Miss Wharton first heard the noise she still remained (calm). (Natural) she felt quite (safe) as she knew that all the doors were (safe) locked. The noise sounded (strange): sometimes like footsteps, sometimes like the scratching of metal on stone. There it was again. Miss Wharton became (restless).

Hers was the last house at the end of Forest Avenue. She could (easy) have kept a dog, but had never felt (nervous) living alone in the old house. The idea of keeping her home (clean) from the invasion of dirt in any form had become quite (obsessive) with her. She was convinced that all dogs smelt (bad) and therefore had (vehement) turned down any suggestion to buy one.

Miss Wharton looked (nervous) at the clock on the bedside table. It was (short) after midnight. Everything remained (quiet). Before Miss Wharton switched out the light she (automatic) felt beside her bed where she (normal) kept the telephone. Her hand grew (stiff) as she (anxious) looked at the thin line of light which (sudden) appeared under the door of her bedroom. It seemed (odd) to her that she had never noticed the gap under the door. Her body turned (cold). She opened her mouth, but her throat felt (dry).

▼ 2. *Write your own version of how the story ends. Use as many adverbs and predicative adjectives as possible.*

B Comparison of Adjectives

133 Refresher Patterns

Regular Comparison

1. Our new house is **smaller.** Its staircase is **narrower,** and its layout is **simpler.** But its kitchen is **roomier,** even though everything else is **compacter.**	Comparison with *-er*, *-est* a) adjectives consisting of 1 syllable b) adjectives consisting of 2 syllables – ending in *-ow*, *-le*, *-y* – with the stress on the 2nd syllable
2. Its location is **more pleasant** and its interior is **more beautiful,** so we are all **more pleased** with our new home.	Comparison with *more*, *most* a) adjectives consisting of 2 syllables with the stress on the 1st syllable b) adjectives consisting of more than 2 syllables c) participles used as adjectives

Irregular Comparison

good	better	best	
bad/ill	worse	worst	
much/many	more	most	
little	smaller	smallest	to denote size *(the smaller of the two)*
little	less	least	to denote quantity (*there is less sugar:* "weniger")
old	older	oldest	*(the oldest house in town)*
old	elder	eldest	used attributively to denote family relationship *(my eldest son)*
late	later	latest	to denote a relationship of time (*the latest news:* "neuest")
	the latter	last	to denote sequence (*the latter:* "der letztere")
near	nearer	nearest	to denote distance *(the nearest hospital)*
		next	to denote sequence *(the next stop)*
far	further	furthest	to denote distance or what comes in addition *(further along the road; further information)*
far	farther	farthest	generally to denote distance *(farther away)*

1.

"The next programme comes via Early Bird and Eurovision links, especially for you."

2.

"Harold is taking a long time finding out where the nearest garage is, mother."

134 A Sales Talk

A car dealer is trying to convince a customer of the extraordinary qualities of the "Rocketeer", the car he wants to sell. He says: "The Rocketeer's engine is more powerful and robuster than any other car's."
Go on with the sales talk. Use the following words:

1. body	stylish; sporty
2. interior	roomy; luxurious
3. seats	wide; soft
4. head-rest	firm; comfortable
5. trunk (boot)	large; practical
6. standard equipment	useful; valuable
7. engine	economical; powerful
8. start	fast; smooth
9. brake system	safe; efficient
10. steering mechanism	simple; convenient
11. ventilation system	good; balanced
12. price	reasonable; low
13. repair service	wide-spread; cheap

135 What Will Become of Pamela?

Choose one of the adjectives given before each paragraph and insert it in the positive, comparative or superlative form, as required.

Pamela's teacher tells her parents:

1. *good/bad* Pamela is ... now in languages but unfortunately still ... than average in science. Her ... tests were those in physics, I'm afraid.
2. *much/many* She obviously hasn't spent ... time on her homework recently, and in ... cases turned up with poor results.
3. *little/few* Pamela often shows very ... interest in the ... things she's got to do. But the ... interest she develops the ... chances she'll have. Very ... pupils realize that there isn't the ... difficulty in achieving the set standards of a first-year physics course.
4. *old/many/good* Can't her ... brother help her as do ... of the ... pupils who have younger sisters and brothers? I think it's one of the ... and certainly ... family traditions that children help each other.
5. *late/much* Pamela shouldn't wait until it's too ... . attempts always take up ... time and energy. Besides, her ... tests have already shown some improvement and it's still quite a while until we do the ... test in the school year.
6. *little/far/good* Her immediate aim should be to reach average standards, at ... Of course, she must try to get ... ahead, because if she's no ... than average, she won't pass her university entrance examination. A concentrated effort from now on will get her ... .

136 A New Block of Flats (Translation)

▼

Suchen Sie eine neue Wohnung? Dann wird Ihnen unser neuestes Projekt gefallen.
In der Victoria Street, einer der ältesten und schönsten Straßen der Stadt, bauen wir ein dreistöckiges Wohnhaus mit den vielen Vorteilen, die die moderne Architektur zu bieten hat: mehr Raum, weniger Lärm, mehr Licht. Die nächste Bushaltestelle ist nur 100 Meter entfernt, und das Einkaufen wird die geringste Ihrer Sorgen sein, denn gleich um die nächste Ecke ist ein Supermarkt.
Wenn Sie weitere Informationen wünschen, schreiben Sie sofort, denn nächste Woche könnte es zu spät sein.

Gebrüder Williams
27, Coventry Road
Lichfield

C Comparison of Adverbs

137 Refresher Patterns

Comparison with *more, most*	**Comparison with** *-er, -est*
We'll get home **more quickly** if we sail this route.	The **faster** we sail, the **further** west we'll get and the **sooner** we'll reach a port.
The comparison with *more, most* is used with all adverbs which end in *-ly.*	The comparison with *-er, -est* is used with 1. adverbs which are identical in form with adjectives (e.g. *fast, hard, long, loud, low, straight*) 2. adverbially used adjectives with irregular comparison (cf. RP, p. 139) 3. some adverbs which are not derived from adjectives (e.g. *soon, early*)

138 Successful Failure

Change the adjectives in brackets into adverbs (c. – comparative; s. – superlative).

No couple had ever practised (long: c.) and (hard: c.) or prepared themselves (thorough: c.) than Mr and Mrs Todd for that spring tournament at Brighton. They couldn't have failed (bad: c.). What all ballroom dancers fear (much: s.) and yet expect (little: s.) happened to the Todds: the spectators began to snigger, then laughed (loud: c.) and (loud: c.) until finally the ballroom burst into uncontrollable laughter. Of course, the Todds had always danced (extravagant: c.) than other couples. But this time they had carried their extravagance (far: c.) than even the most tolerant judge would accept. "The (soon: c.) they give up, the (good: c.)!" one of them was overheard saying.

Today *The Toddlers*, alias Mr and Mrs Todd, are the (good: s.) paid comic dancers in England and the USA. Within the last two years their fame on TV has grown (fast: c.) than that of all other comedians. Most experts agree that in recent years no one has promoted the art of parody and pantomime (successful: c.) than *The Toddlers.*

Annotations
tournament ['tuənəmənt] – **to snigger** kichern – **alias** ['eiliæs] – **comedian** [kə'mi:djən] actor in comedies – **to promote s. th.** to help the progress of s.th., to make s.th. a success.

139 Polar Tragedy (Translation)

1. Von allen Expeditionen zum Südpol endete Captain Scotts Expedition im Jahre 1912 am tragischsten.
2. Was er eine Zeitlang am meisten befürchtet und dennoch am wenigsten erwartet hatte, geschah tatsächlich.
3. Der Norweger Amundsen erreichte den Pol einen Monat früher als Scott.
4. Nichts hätte die britische Mannschaft tiefer enttäuschen können als diese Entdeckung.
5. Amundsen hatte das Transportproblem wirksamer gelöst als Scott.
6. Die Hunde, die er zum Ziehen der Schlitten (sledge) benutzte, bewegten sich viel schneller und konnten natürliche Hindernisse leichter umgehen als Scotts Ponys.
7. Scotts Männer hofften schließlich, daß, je eher sie die Ponys loswürden, sie desto besser vorankommen würden.
8. Aber nachdem sie die Ponys erschossen hatten, mußten die Männer noch härter kämpfen als zuvor.
9. Auf ihrem Rückweg vom Pol litten sie unter Erfrierungen (frostbite – *singular*), die sie zwangen, immer öfter anzuhalten.
10. Schließlich häufte (pile up) ein schwerer Sturm den Schnee immer höher um das kleine Zelt, in das die letzten drei Überlebenden (survivor) gekrochen waren und wo sie den Tod fanden.

D Adjectives as Nouns – Adjectives with Prop-words

140 Refresher Patterns

1. **The young** often reach out for **the impossible.**	**The definite article + adjective** (never with plural "s") to denote a) a whole group of persons b) a quality in the abstract
2. However, *an* **old man** who has lived a full life and even *some* **young people,** too, may say the **most important thing** *in their lives* is to have done something useful.	To denote a) individual persons b) a limited group c) a quality in the abstract which is more closely defined the adjective must be followed by a **prop-word,** e.g. *man*, *woman*, *person*, *thing*, *one* (or their plurals), *people*
3. Tolerance can help understanding between *an old person* and *a young* **one.**	*one(s)* is used to avoid the repetition of a noun, for stylistic reasons

Note: Adjectives and participles used as abstract nouns are much more frequent in German than in English; e.g.

"das Neue an der Sache war"	the new element was/what was new
"das Erreichte"	what has been achieved/was achieved
"das Störende"	what disturbed me/us

"At least there's not one law for the rich and another for the poor!"

141 The Good and the Clever

If only the good were the clever,
  If only the clever were good,
The world would be better than ever
  We thought that it possibly could.

But, alas, it is seldom or never
  That either behave as they should;
For the good are so harsh to the clever,
  The clever so rude to the good.

Attributed to Elizabeth Wordsworth (1840–1932)

1. *Translate the poem.*
2. *Say who the good and the clever mentioned in the poem may be. Try and explain the poem.*

142 The Generation Gap (Translation)

▼ 1. Das Auffallende (striking) bei vielen Erwachsenen ist ihre Unfähigkeit, die Jungen zu verstehen.
2. Diese Haltung kann man sowohl bei (among) Reichen als auch bei Armen beobachten.
3. Oft scheinen die Älteren die Verbindung sogar mit den Jüngeren zu verlieren, die zu ihrer eigenen sozialen Schicht gehören.
4. Dies geschieht besonders deshalb, weil sie am Traditionellen hängen (cling to) und gewöhnlich nicht gewillt sind, Modernes zu akzeptieren.
5. Die Jungen dagegen wollen nicht so sehr über das Vergangene nachdenken; sie wollen lieber über das Zukünftige diskutieren.
6. Das Wichtigste, wenn man sich mit jungen Menschen beschäftigt, ist zu verstehen, was ihre wahren Absichten oft sind: für das Gemeinwohl (das gemeinsame Gute) zu arbeiten und die Ehrgeizigen und Skrupellosen (unscrupulous) daran zu hindern, die Schwachen auszubeuten.

143 Utopia

In his utopia *Brave New World* Aldous Huxley describes a world-state, in which medicine and science have achieved the impossible: the conquest of disease and old age. Sickness doesn't exist any more in this utopia and a man in his old age doesn't look any different from a young one.

Hormones, magnesium salts, and the transfusion of young blood enable the old to keep their physical and mental powers. Nobody, however, is allowed to grow older than seventy. Towards the end of their lifetime the old are sent to a "hospital" for the dying. The astonishing thing about this is that they go quite willingly because in *Brave New World*, from the age of 18 months on, the young are sent to these "hospitals" twice a week in order to be death-conditioned. By watching the dying they learn to take death as a matter of course.

But in *Brave New World* even the dead are socially and materially useful: the living gain phosphorus from their bodies which is then used to make plants grow.

The amazing thing about this book, written in 1932, is that, far from presenting the improbable, it describes projects of which particularly many technical ones have been realized in the meantime. Nowadays, for example, the sick have a better chance of being cured than ever before. Medicine can help many sick people who suffer from organic trouble by means of heart, liver, and kidney transplantations. The unbelievable may very well happen: at some stage in the future sickness may have been completely overcome.

1. *Say what happens to the various groups of people in Huxley's* Brave New World *as described in the text. Use adjectives as nouns in your answers.*
2. *Make a list of all the adjectives which are used*
   a) *as nouns,*
   b) *together with prop-words.*
3. *Explain in each case why the prop-word is necessary or not (cf. RP, p. 144).*

E Types and Positions of Adverbs /Adverbials

144 Refresher Patterns

	Types of Adverbials	Positions
1. a) Many young people were **eagerly** expecting the first London concert of "The Jollies." b) **Naturally** all of them wanted to go there. c) The time before the concert passed **slowly.**	of manner or viewpoint (e.g. *slowly*, *happily*, *well*, *fast*, *obviously*, *of course)*	a) before the main verb b) front-position (often for special emphasis) c) end-position (often for special emphasis, or if the sentence has no object)
2. a) All the tickets were **soon** sold out. b) **Several times** the police had to be called. c) They managed to get the crowd under control **eventually.**	of frequency or indefinite time (e.g. *already*, *sometimes*, *often)*	a) before the main verb b) front-position (often for special emphasis) c) end-position (often for special emphasis)
3. a) **All day long** people kept asking for tickets **at the Palladium.** b) **At the Palladium** people kept asking for tickets **all day long.**	of place and (definite) time (e.g. *there*, *at the bus stop*, *tomorrow*, *at 4 o'clock)*	a) front- or end-position b) front-position of the adverbial of place: for special emphasis
4. The audience were **completely** hysterical when the concert began.	of degree (e.g. *rather*, *very*, *quite*, *nearly*)	before the word which it qualifies

Note: Adverbials may be adverbs *(fast)*, adverbial phrases *(at five o'clock)*, adverbial clauses *(when he came home)*.

1. 

"We'll have to find another excuse to meet secretly."

2. 

"Then my lawyer said, morally you've won the case, legally you've got fifteen years."

145 The Ballad of Grand Canyon

Insert the adverbials given in brackets.

When my brother Alan and I were touring the USA, people told us that we must see Grand Canyon (a few years ago; again and again; really). We didn't want to miss what has been called "God's masterpiece" (naturally; often). We arrived and decided to explore the bottom of the Canyon on mule-back (at the Canyon; on Easter Day). The group we joined consisted of twelve tourists who were looking forward to an exciting adventure (the next morning; eagerly). We were no expert riders but we were confident when we set out (certainly; fairly). However, we discovered that this was not going to be a mere pleasure-trip (soon, definitely). My mule started falling behind and I had to work in order to make her move (at once; hard; more quickly). This was tiring and prevented me from enjoying the beauties of the Canyon (extremely, naturally).

Alan had a different kind of problem (completely): his mule didn't stay in the middle of the trail but balanced on the edge of it, which made Alan sick with fear of falling into the depths of the Canyon (dangerously; absolutely). Every single muscle began to ache (after an hour; terribly). The Canyon had lost its attraction for us (entirely). We were hanging in the saddle, trying to find a more comfortable way of sitting (weakly; desperately). When our ordeal was over, we had all changed our opinion about those Western heroes who spent their lives in the saddle (after eight hours; finally; drastically; light-heartedly).

146 Sleep, Sweet Sleep

1. *Insert the adverbials given in brackets.*

   a) The people upstairs go to bed before one o'clock (never).
   b) But before they retire the husband takes the dog out (just; always).
   c) It's a wild boxer which begins to bark once it's outside their apartment (extremely; immediately).
   d) The owner of the dog forgets his key (almost; regularly).
   e) He rings the bell. He calls his wife (frequently; occasionally).
   f) She slams up the window and shouts, "What's the matter, darling?" (noisily; at the top of her voice).
   g) She throws down the key which gets lost among the bushes in the front garden (then; naturally).
   h) The man begins to curse, the dog howls (angrily; miserably).
   i) Husband, wife, and dog are reunited (eventually).
   j) The noises die down and I fall asleep (gradually; at last).

2. **"sehr"**

The night was **very** *quiet.* **Very** *gently* the wind blew through the trees.	The sudden roaring of a car *annoyed* us **very much.**
very modifies adjectives or adverbs	*very much* modifies verbs

3. **Translation**

   a) Im allgemeinen mag ich unser Haus sehr.
   b) Es steht in einer sehr ruhigen Straße mit sehr alten Bäumen.
   c) Persönlich schätze ich diese Ruhe sehr, da ich sehr oft zu Hause arbeite.
   d) Viele meiner Nachbarn hingegen gehen sehr früh am Morgen weg oder kommen sehr spät am Abend wieder.
   e) Einige der älteren Häuser in unserer Straße wurden letztes Jahr sehr geschickt renoviert.
   f) Nun beeindrucken sie Besucher unseres Stadtteils wieder sehr.

147 The Armchair Champion

Make use of the adverbials given under each picture to describe what happens:
"Mr MacDonald is standing ..."

in front of a TV shop
with great excitement
admiringly

fired with enthusiasm
happily

energetically
at a time

elegantly
onto the hook

into his slippers
skilfully

finally
peacefully

148 The End is Near

▼ My grandfather used to travel from school to school where he displayed all kinds of animals and gave lectures on them. He had an old car which was piled with cages of rabbits, hamsters, rats, mice and birds, bowls of fish and boxes of snakes. I was allowed to accompany him.

We took the car ferry to Lemon Island. The car was parked on the deck. The sea was smooth and we decided that we could leave the animals. We strolled about the boat resting on the benches along the railing, and dropped in at the ferry's little bar for a drink and an ice-cream.

We returned to the car and noticed one of the ferry's officers staring at the vehicle. "Anything wrong?" Grandfather inquired. The officer shook his head keeping his eyes fixed on the little zoo inside the car. "That your car?" he muttered. "Why, yes," Grandfather replied. The officer turned and looked Grandfather over. "Your name isn't Noah?" he said.

Go over the text again and add adverbials wherever suitable. Start like this: "Many years ago my grandfather ..."

149 Two Kinds of Prose

1. I wakened quickly and sat up in bed abruptly. It is only when I am anxious that I waken easily and for a minute I did not know why my heart was beating faster than usual. Then I remembered. The old reason. He had not come home.

   Getting out I rested for a moment on the edge of the bed, smoothing the green satin bedspread with my hand. We had forgotten to fold it the previous night, Mama and me. Slowly I slid on to the floor and the linoleum was cold on the soles of my feet. My toes curled up instinctively ...

   I put on my ankle socks.

   There was a smell of frying bacon from the kitchen, but it didn't cheer me.

   Then I went over to let up the blind. It shot up suddenly and the cord got twisted round it. It was lucky that Mama had gone downstairs, as she was always lecturing me on how to let up blinds properly, gently.

From *The Country Girls*, by Edna O'Brien. Hutchinson Publishing Group Ltd., London

2. The old man looked at him. "Another brandy," he said.

   "You'll be drunk," the waiter said. The old man looked at him. The waiter went away.

"He'll stay all night," he said to his colleague. "I'm sleepy now. I never get to bed before three o'clock. He should have killed himself last week."

The waiter took the brandy bottle and another saucer from the counter inside the café and marched out to the old man's table. He put down the saucer and poured the glass full of brandy.

"You should have killed yourself last week," he said to the deaf man. The old man motioned with his finger. "A little more," he said. The waiter poured on into the glass so that the brandy slopped over and ran down the stem into the top saucer of the pile. "Thank you," the old man said. The waiter took the bottle back inside the café. He sat down at the table with his colleague again.

From *A Clean, Well-lighted Place*, by Ernest Hemingway. In: *The Short Happy Life of Francis Macomber and Other Stories.* © Estate of Ernest Hemingway.

3. *What kind of adverb is used frequently in text 1 and is completely lacking in text 2? (Cf. RP, p. 148)*
4. *Describe how this affects the style and atmosphere of the texts.*

150 The 800th Lifetime

1. **The Word Order in Sentences with Negative or Restrictive Adverbials**

1. Man has **never** used so many material goods as in our lifetime.	When the adverbial is used non-emphatically, it is placed before the main verb.
2. a) **Never** has man used so many material goods as in our lifetime.	When the adverbial is used with special emphasis, it is placed at the beginning of the sentence, which makes inversion necessary.
2. b) **Never** *did* man use so many material goods as in our lifetime.	When there is no auxiliary, a form of *to do* has to be used.

2. It has been observed that if the last 50,000 years of man's existence were divided into lifetimes of approximately sixty-two years each, there have been about 800 such lifetimes. Of these 800, fully 650 were spent in caves. Only during the last seventy lifetimes has it been possible to communicate effectively

from one lifetime to another – as writing made it possible to do. Only during the last six lifetimes did masses of men ever see a printed word. Only during the last four has it been possible to measure time with any precision. Only in the last two has anyone anywhere used an electric motor. And the overwhelming majority of all the material goods we use in daily life today have been developed within the present, the 800th, lifetime.

3. *Read the four sentences in text 2 beginning with* only *once more and explain the sentence structure; why is* did *used in l. 6*?
4. *Use the following phrases to say what man did not achieve until this lifetime. Begin your sentences with* Never before ...
   a) to fly from continent to continent in a few hours
   b) to travel faster than sound
   c) to explore space by satellite
   d) to fly into space
   e) to land on the moon
5. *Use the following phrases to say what has become possible in our lifetime. Begin your sentences with* Only during our lifetime ...
   a) to witness events in distant countries
   b) to build jumbo jets
   c) to reach other planets
   d) to invent the computer
   e) to have the power to destroy Earth by H-bombs

Relative Clauses

151 Refresher Patterns

1. Defining relative clauses (without commas)

a) The teacher **who taught us German** was called Mr Wheatler.	a) Defining relative clauses give information which is necessary to make the meaning of a statement clear.
b) Mr Wheatler was the teacher **(who/whom/that)** we liked best and German became the subject **(which/that)** we enjoyed most.	b) In spoken English the relative pronoun is usually omitted when it is the object of a defining relative clause.
c) His methods included *everything* **that** made learning interesting. German was the *only* subject **that** was really popular with us.	c) *that* is used only in defining relative clauses; it is preferred after *only*, *all*, *everything*, *something*, *anything*, superlatives, *first*, *last*.
d) Wheatler was the only teacher **(that)** no one ever complained **about.**	d) Prepositions must be placed at the end of the clause if the relative pronoun is omitted or if it is *that*.
e) He was a person **in whom** we always put our trust./He was a person **who/whom** we always put our trust **in.**	e) In other cases prepositions may be placed at the beginning or at the end of the clause.

2. Non-defining relative clauses (with commas)

a) French, **which was our second foreign language,** was never so popular.	a) Non-defining relative clauses (used almost only in written English) give additional information.
b) I can still understand quite a lot of German, **which** is not the case with French.	b) *which* in the meaning of German "was" refers to a whole sentence.
c) My French, **in which** I failed most exams, was always poor.	c) Prepositions in non-defining relative clauses are usually placed before the relative pronoun.

Note: "das was": **What** we liked most about him was his sense of humour.
"alles was": I can remember **all (that)/everything (that)** he taught us.

1.

"No, if you've only been working here two days, it couldn't have been you who took my order!"

2.

"I assure you, sir, it's not the same steak you sent back, *he's* eating that!"

152 Ken's Dream

Put in relative pronouns where necessary.

Ken Tu Me is the only person ... I know ... learned to drive a car not *from* books but *on* books. I met Ken at the American university ... we had both got scholarships from. He was a South Korean and about half the size of his huge American fellow-students, a fact ... caused the following incident, ... I'll never forget.

One day Ken achieved ... he had always dreamt of: he bought the biggest second-hand car ... he could get his hands on, a monster of a thing, in ... Ken's tiny figure almost completely disappeared. As he could only look *through* its over-sized steering-wheel and not *over* it, he put several books on the seat, ... increased his field of vision by about 85%.

On a ride to ... he had invited me he unfortunately chose to cross the only railroad track ... led through our town. At the first jolt something happened ... gave our trip a dramatic turn: the books slipped from under him and Ken lost control of vision, steering-wheel and everything else. The car, ... somehow got caught up in the rails, ran along the track until it came to a gradual stop. We did ... was the most reasonable thing ... we could do in the situation: we jumped out – just a few seconds before the 12.15 Santa Fé Express heading for Kansas City hit Ken's "dream".

153 Definitions

What is an enemy? *Militarily* the answer is clear: It is the armed forces of a nation with which there is overt or latent hostility which might lead to war. *Politically* an enemy is harder to define but refers to those who are in the "opposition" or those who oppose "our" power aspirations. *Socially* the enemy consists of one's foes, those whom we feel are trying to harm or attack us, or those toward whom we have ill-feelings or hatred.

Generally, the idea of the enemy connotes something or someone we perceive to be threatening or harmful to our welfare or wishes. More particularly, we perceive malice in the acts or intentions of another party. It is a result, then, of our view of those intentions and activities which leads us to consider another as an enemy.

From *Enemies in Politics*, by David J. Finlay.

Annotations

overt ['əuvə:t] open – **latent** ['leitənt] present but not visible – **aspiration** desire – **foe** [fəu] enemy – **to connote** [kə'nəut] to mean also – **malice** ['mælis] unfriendly feelings

1. *The text contains many relative clauses. What is the author's aim in using them?*

2. *Explain each relative clause according to the* *Refresher Patterns, p. 155.*

3. *Use relative clauses to define or explain the following terms:*
   a) manager
   b) talkshow
   c) band
   d) fan
   e) jeans

▼ 4. *Imagine you had to explain to an English-speaking person the following German terms. Use relative clauses.*
   a) Gemütlichkeit
   b) Tüchtigkeit
   c) Weltanschauung
   d) Bürgerinitiative
   e) Lieschen Müller

154 Non-conformists

▼ *Complete the text by inserting suitable relative clauses.*

1. We call those people ... non-conformists.
2. For instance, the trends in fashion ... are completely ignored by them.
3. Many people are annoyed at ... and either despise or discriminate against them.
4. Nevertheless, true non-conformists will only do ... no matter what everyone else does.
5. Anything ... is irrelevant to them.
6. The goals in life ... don't mean much to them.
7. To achieve security, something ... is of no interest to them.
8. To be informed about ... is of no importance to them.
9. The last thing ... is to live like everyone else.
10. All ... is proving their originality.

155 Comparing Texts

I had lately returned to London from China and was having tea with Mrs Tower. Mrs Tower had been seized with the passion for decoration; and had sacrificed chairs in which she had comfortably sat for years, pictures that had been familiar to her for a generation; and delivered herself into the hands of an expert. Nothing remained in her drawing-room with which she had any association, or to which any sentiment was attached; and she invited me that day to see the fashionable glory in which she now lived. Everything that could be pickled was pickled and what couldn't be pickled was painted.

The room was beautiful, yet to me it lacked something. I wondered what it was that I missed in all these rooms that the decorators were turning out with a profitable industry. Was it heart? But Mrs Tower looked about her happily.

"Don't you like my alabaster lamps?" she said. "They give such a soft light." "Personally I have a weakness for a light that you can see by," I smiled. "It's so difficult to combine that with a light that you can't be too much seen by," laughed Mrs Tower.

Annotations

decoration *here:* the furnishing of rooms – **to attach sentiment to** to have tender feelings for – **pickled** gebeizt

1. *Explain the different kinds of relative clauses used in the text (cf. RP, p. 155).*

2. *Pick out those sentences in which the relative pronouns could be left out and read out the new versions.*

Then we started fighting and I slipped and he had me down kneeling on my chest and choking me with both hands like he was trying to kill me and all the time I was trying to get the knife out of my pocket to cut him loose. Everybody was too drunk to pull him off me. He was choking me and hammering my head on the floor and I got the knife out and opened it up; and I cut the muscle right across his arm and he let go of me. He couldn't have held on if he wanted to. Then he rolled and hung on to that arm and started to cry and I said: "What the hell you want to choke me for?"

I'd have killed him. I couldn't swallow for a week. He hurt my throat bad.

▼ 3. *The passage from Maugham's story contains eleven relative clauses, the one from Hemingway none at all. This gives each text a different character. Try to explain the difference.*

Acknowledgements

Daily Mirror: p. 16,1 and 2; p. 21,2; p. 26,1 and 2; p. 34,1 and 2; p. 42,2; p. 50,1,2 and 3; p. 56,1 and 2; p. 59; p. 62,1 and 2; p. 80; p. 87,1 and 2; p. 91,1 and 2; p. 95,1 and 2; p. 99; p. 104,1 and 2; p. 109,1 and 2; p. 116,1 and 2; p. 120; p. 124,1 and 2; p. 129,1; p. 133,1; p. 137,1 and 2; p. 140,1 and 2; p. 149,1 and 2; p. 156,1 and 2; Love Story (pp. 36–37) from *Rien n'est simple* by Sempé; Pick of Punch, 1960: pp. 67–68; Pick of Punch, 1961: p. 10; p. 112; Pick of Punch, 1964: p. 18; p. 83; p. 145; Punch, 28th April 1976: p. 20; 22nd March 1967: p. 21,1; 6th April 1960: p. 42,1; 3rd December 1969: p. 46; 22nd May 1968: p. 53; 7th November 1973: p. 74; 6th March 1974: p. 77; 19th March 1975: p. 129,2; Ronald Searle (p. 133,2) © 1960, from *The Penguin Ronald Searle*, Penguin Books Ltd.; Show Jumping (p. 55) from *A Leg at Each Corner* by Norman Thelwell, published by Eyre Methuen Ltd.; The Armchair Champion (p. 151) from *Sauve qui peut* by Sempé; The Eye-catcher (p. 13) from *Cobean's Naked Eye* by Sam Cobean. © 1950 by Sam Cobean, by permission of Harper & Row, Publishers, Inc. Repeated attempts to trace the copyright holders of the Elizabeth Wordsworth poem (p. 145) were unsuccessful.

Learning English A4/B3
Modern Life

Lese- und Arbeitsbuch für die Ober- und Studienstufe

Herausgegeben von H.-J. Lechler und F. Ungerer unter Mitarbeit von G. Fisch und J. W. Gerhards.

In 9 Kapiteln werden die Stoffkreise *Views and Voices, The Arts, Language, Mass Media, Social Problems, Politics, Business, Science, Our Environment* behandelt. Vom Brief bis zum Interview, vom Inserat bis zum Filmscript, vom Pamphlet bis zum *radio talk,* vom Einakter bis zum wissenschaftlichen Bericht wird ein Fächer sprachlicher Register angeboten, an dem der Schüler die Vielschichtigkeit des Englischen erfährt. Die Texte greifen die Problematik unserer modernen Gesellschaft auf und sprechen den jungen Menschen in seinen eigenen Interessen an.

Einsprachige Wort- und Sacherklärungen, ein ausführlicher Apparat von Verständnisfragen, Diskussionsstoffen und übergreifenden Aufgaben machen das Werk zum Arbeitsbuch und leisten sowohl dem Lehrer als auch dem Schüler eine entscheidende Hilfe bei der Texterschließung. Die Vielfalt der Aufgaben ermöglicht Gruppenarbeit, Kurzreferate, Facharbeiten und andere Formen selbständiger Arbeit, mit denen im Zuge der Oberstufenreform die Schüler zur Arbeitsweise der Universität hingeführt werden sollen.

Lese- und Arbeitsbuch, Klettbuch 5084
Teacher's Book, Klettbuch 50843
3 Schallplatten, 17 cm ø, 33 U/min, Klettnummer 50841
Compact-Cassette, Sprechzeit ca. 43 min, Klettnummer 50847
1 Tonband, Sprechzeit ca. 43 min, Klettnummer 50848

Hauke Kock

Das will ich wissen

Die Wikinger

Hauke Kock

ist Jahrgang 1965 und studierte Kommunikations-Design. Seit 1991 arbeitet er als freischaffender Illustrator. Er illustriert vor allem Kinder- und Jugendsachbücher. Nebenher interessiert er sich für freie Malerei und Fotografie. Außerdem beschäftigt er sich viel mit der Geschichte der Wikinger. Für Arena hat er dieses Buch geschrieben und illustriert.

Hauke Kock

Das will ich wissen

Die Wikinger

Arena

In neuer Rechtschreibung

***

Sonderausgabe 2008

Einband und Innenillustrationen: Hauke Kock
Gesamtherstellung: Westermann Druck Zwickau GmbH
ISBN 978-3-401-06284-6

www.arena-verlag.de

Inhalt

Die Fahrt nach Haithabu

Hildigunn ist aufgeregt: In diesem Frühjahr darf sie zum ersten Mal ihren Vater Olof nach Haithabu begleiten. Hildigunns Vater ist ein Waffenschmied, der Schwerter, Äxte und Helme herstellt. An diesem schönen Sommermorgen beladen die Dorfbewohner ein Schiff mit Waren, die sie in der großen Stadt verkaufen wollen.
Hildigunns Mutter steht am Ufer.
»Alles Gute für die Reise. Möge Thor euch beschützen!«, ruft sie.

Bei günstigem Wind stechen die Wikinger in See. Olof steht am Ruder. Er kennt die Route am besten, denn er ist schon oft nach Haithabu gefahren. Nachdem sie einige Zeit an der Küste entlanggesegelt sind, steuert das Schiff aufs offene Meer hinaus. Schon bald ist kein Land mehr zu sehen. Das Geschaukel auf dem Schiff hat Hildigunn müde gemacht. Sie schläft ein. Als sie am nächsten Morgen früh erwacht, fahren sie in den Hafen von Haithabu ein.

Ihr Schiff legt an einem der Holzstege an.
Olof winkt einem Mann zu.
»Das ist mein Bruder Snorri«, sagt er freudig.
»Dein Onkel. Er lebt hier. Und sieh nur,
er hat seinen Sohn Bjarni mitgebracht!«
Die beiden Männer begrüßen sich.
Während sie von alten Zeiten und den
Geschäften reden, fragt Bjarni das Mädchen:
»Möchtest du, dass ich dir die Stadt zeige?«
Hildigunn nickt.
»Dann komm mit.«

Und was für eine Stadt das ist! Hildigunn hat noch nie so viele Häuser und Menschen gesehen wie in Haithabu. In den schmalen Gassen, die mit Holzbohlen befestigt sind, herrscht ein lautes Geschiebe und Gedränge. Die Leute sprechen in vielen Sprachen durcheinander.

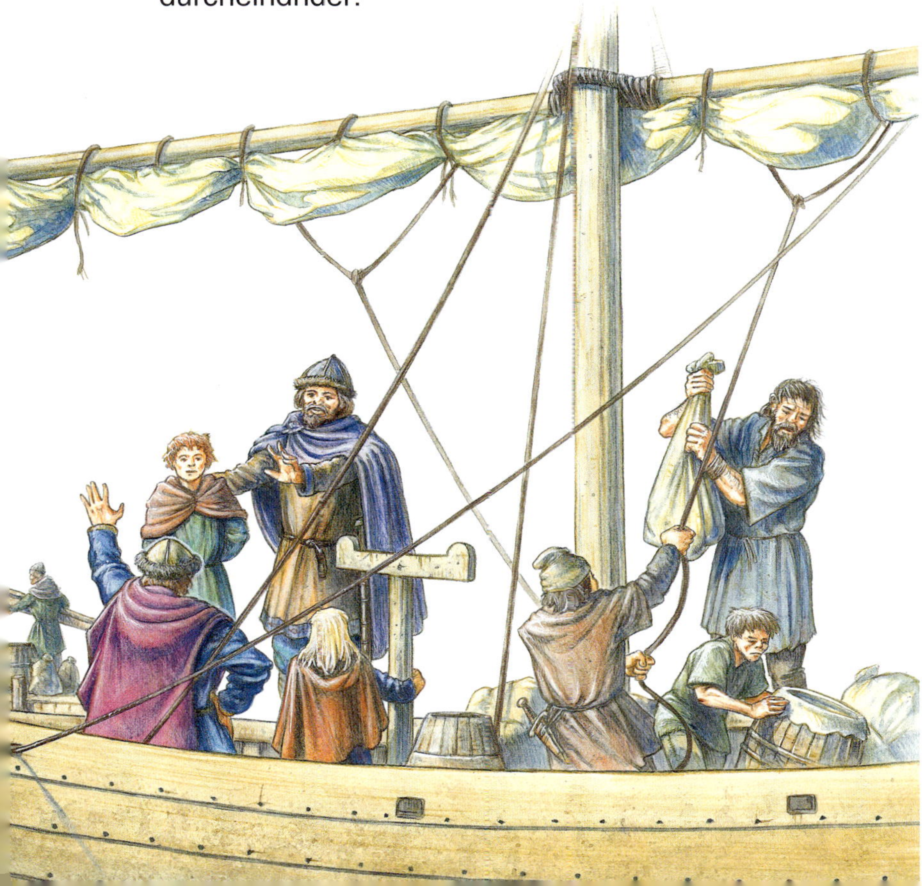

»Wo kommen die denn bloß alle her?«, fragt Hildigunn. Bjarni erklärt es ihr. »Hier in Haithabu leben viele Kaufleute aus aller Herren Länder. Friesen und Franken, Sachsen und Slawen kannst du hier treffen. Und sieh mal den da: ein Araber aus dem fernen Kalifat.«

Hildigunn kommt aus dem Staunen nicht heraus. Und was es alles zu kaufen gibt! Bjarni zeigt ihr Walrosselfenbein aus Grönland, Bernsteine von der baltischen Küste, norwegischen Speckstein, feine Tuche aus Friesland, Töpferwaren, Honig, Ketten aus glitzernden Glasperlen, wertvolle Pelze, bunt gefärbte Mäntel aus Schafswolle, herrlichen Schmuck.

Am besten gefallen ihr die schönen, aus Geweih geschnitzten Kämme.

Hildigunn sieht auch die Sklaven, die von wohlhabenden Wikingern gekauft werden. Sie ist sehr froh, keine Sklavin zu sein!

Klappwaage
mit Gewichten

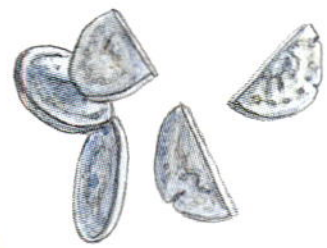

Hacksilber

Bjarni deutet auf ein paar Händler. Sie wiegen das Silber, mit dem man hier bezahlt, auf einer kleinen Waage. Ist das Gewicht für den ausgehandelten Kaufpreis zu hoch, hacken sie einfach ein Stück von der Silbermünze ab.
Den ganzen Tag streifen die Kinder zwischen den Häusern umher. Sie steigen auf den Erdwall, der die Stadt zum Schutz umgibt, und schauen über die Dächer.

Als es zu dämmern beginnt, gehen sie in Bjarnis Haus. Snorri und Olof sind schon da und kosten vom Met. Hildigunns Vater ist bester Laune. Er hat gut gehandelt und alle seine Waren für viel Silber verkauft.
»Sieh mal, was ich hier für dich habe«, sagt er und zieht etwas aus seiner Tasche. Es ist ein feiner, verzierter Kamm aus Hirschhorn. Das ist der schönste Kamm, den Hildigunn je gesehen hat.

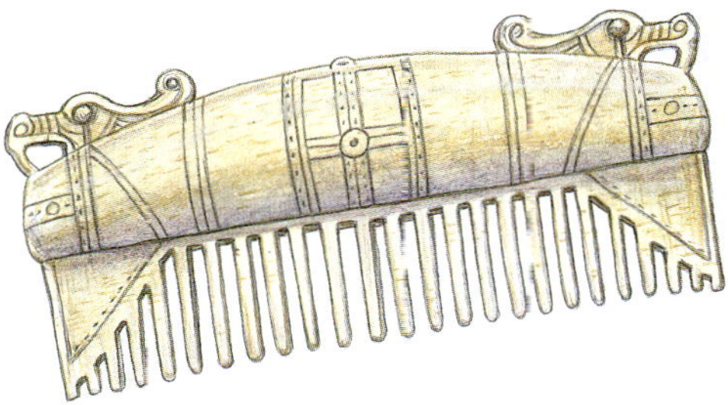

Die Wikingerzeit

Die Wikinger lebten im frühen Mittelalter.
Sie stammen aus Skandinavien. Das sind die Länder, die wir heute Dänemark, Norwegen und Schweden nennen.
Das altnordische Wort »vikingr« bedeutet »Seeräuber«. Die Menschen in ganz Europa erzitterten vor Angst beim Klang dieses Namens.
Doch die Wikinger waren nicht nur gefürchtete Krieger. Sie waren auch kühne Entdecker, fleißige Händler und reiche Kaufleute, geschickte Handwerker und mutige Siedler.

Sie reisten weit über die Grenzen der damals bekannten Welt hinaus. Ihre Segelschiffe durchpflügten die Wellen des Nordatlantiks. Die Wikinger erforschten unentdeckte Inseln und fremde Küsten.

Wo es ihnen gefiel, ließen sie sich als Händler, Bauern oder Jäger nieder. Sie gründeten neue Städte und machtvolle Staaten fern ihrer alten Heimat.

Überfall!

An einem Junitag des Jahres 793 tauchten Segel am Horizont vor der Ostküste Englands auf. Die Mönche des nahen Klosters Lindisfarne hegten keinen Argwohn. Schließlich war Lindisfarne ein heiliger Wallfahrtsort.
Doch jene fremdartigen Schiffe trugen Furcht einflößende Drachenköpfe und ihre Besatzung bestand aus starken, bewaffneten Kämpfern.

Die Fremden stürmten an Land. Sie erschlugen die Mönche und raubten die Schätze des Klosters. Sie plünderten die Vorratskammern und schlachteten das Vieh.
Dann luden die Krieger die Beute auf ihre Schiffe und verschwanden so plötzlich, wie sie aufgetaucht waren.
Die Kunde dieser Gräueltat verbreitete sich rasch in ganz Europa. Überall erklang ein neues Gebet: »Oh Herr, errette uns vor der Raserei der Nordmänner.«

Der Überfall auf Lindisfarne war erst der Anfang. Wikinger wurden bald an allen Küsten Europas gefürchtet. Wo ihre Drachenschiffe auftauchten, herrschten Angst und Panik. Über die Flüsse drangen die Wikinger weiter ins Landesinnere vor, um dort Klöster, Kirchen und Städte zu berauben und zu brandschatzen.

Viele Städte und Landstriche hatten unter den Beutezügen der Wikinger zu leiden: Hamburg und Aachen, Rouen, Orléans und Paris, York und die irische Küste, Sevilla in Spanien, sogar das ferne Konstantinopel (Istanbul). Dann überließ im Jahr 911 Karl der Einfältige, der König des Westfränkischen Reichs, dem Wikingerfürsten Rollo ein Gebiet. Noch heute nennen wir es nach den Nordmännern »Normandie«. Dafür ließen sich die »heidnischen« Wikinger taufen und beschützten von da ab die Küste des westlichen Frankenreiches, das wir heute Frankreich nennen.

Geniale Schiffsbauer

Die Erfolge der Wikinger wären ohne ihre überlegenen Kenntnisse im Schiffsbau undenkbar gewesen. Hier wird gerade ein Langschiff gebaut. Das war ein schnelles, schlankes und wendiges Kriegsschiff.
Es wurde gesegelt oder von Ruderern fortbewegt. Damit konnten die Wikinger auch in flachen Küstengewässern oder in Flüssen manövrieren. Die Schiffswände wurden mit den runden Schilden der Wikinger verziert.

Auf Kriegsfahrten wurden hölzerne, geschnitzte Drachenköpfe am Schiffsbug angebracht.
Sie sollten die Feinde erschrecken.
Daher kommt auch der Name »Drachenschiff«.

Drachenschiff

Sonnenkompass

Knorr

Ein anderer Schiffstyp der Wikinger war der Knorr. Damit konnten die Wikinger weiter, schneller und sicherer als ihre Zeitgenossen reisen.

Meistens fuhren sie in Küstennähe. Wenn sie über das offene Meer segelten, orientierten sich die Seeleute am Sonnenstand oder an der Position der Sterne.

Auf solche Schiffe luden die Wikinger ihr Vieh
und all ihr Hab und Gut. Dann nahmen sie ihre
Familien an Bord und machten sich auf,
um neue Inseln und unentdeckte Landstriche
zu besiedeln.

Auf zu neuen Ufern

Solche Wikinger, die ins Ungewisse fuhren und sich auf entlegenen und unwirtlichen Inseln niederließen, waren keine Krieger.
Sie waren Bauern und suchten neues Siedlungsland, weil es ihnen in Skandinavien zu eng wurde oder sie Probleme mit den dortigen Herrschern hatten.

Diese Wikinger ließen sich auf Island nieder, wo sie ein freies Leben ohne König führten.
Jedes Jahr traf sich die Bevölkerung zum Althing, der großen Ratsversammlung.
Dort wurden Gesetze erlassen, Gerichtstage abgehalten und Urteile gefällt.

Erik der Rote, ein von Island verbannter Wikinger, segelte mit einigen Gefolgsleuten sogar noch weiter nach Westen.
Dort wurde eine neue Insel entdeckt, die Erik »Grünes Land« taufte. So nannte er sie, um viele Siedler zum Mitkommen zu bewegen.
Heute kennen wir die Insel unter dem Namen Grönland.
Hier lebten die Wikinger von der Viehzucht, dem Fischfang und der Jagd nach Walen, Robben, Eisbären und Walrössern.

Die Wikinger auf Grönland hörten durch andere Seefahrer von Ländern noch weiter im Westen. Also rüstete um das Jahr 987 der Sohn Eriks des Roten, Leif Eriksson, ein Schiff aus und stach in See.
Bald erreichte Leif mit seinen Begleitern fremde Küsten: das karge »Helluland«, das waldreiche »Markland« und »Vinland«. Damit waren die Wikinger mehr als 500 Jahre vor Kolumbus in Amerika!

Später kamen noch andere Grönländer nach Vinland und siedelten sich dort an.
Die Wikinger trafen auf ein Volk, das sie »Skraelinge« nannten. Heute bezeichnen wir diese Volksstämme als Indianer.
Zuerst kamen die Wikinger und die Ureinwohner gut miteinander aus. Sie führten regen Tauschhandel.
Doch bald gab es Streit und blutige Kämpfe.
Deswegen gaben die Wikinger nach wenigen Jahren ihre Versuche auf, dauerhaft in Amerika sesshaft zu werden.

Auch im Osten suchten die Wikinger ihr Glück. Das waren vor allem die schwedischen Wikinger. Sie ließen sich an der baltischen Küste nieder und befuhren die großen Flüsse des Slawenlandes. Dabei gelangten sie bis zum Schwarzen Meer und bis zur Seidenstraße. Sie unterhielten sogar Handelsbeziehungen mit dem Kalifen von Bagdad.
Die Wikinger wurden von den einheimischen Slawen »Rus« genannt. Da sie als Händler und nicht als Eroberer kamen, wurden sie von der Bevölkerung gut aufgenommen. Sie bildeten mit der Hauptstadt Kiew das Reich der Rus – der Ursprung des heutigen Russlands.

Auch Konstantinopel, die Hauptstadt des Oströmischen Reiches, war ein Ziel der Wikinger. Dort nannte man sie »Waräger«. Der Kaiser von Konstantinopel bot ihnen wegen ihres berühmten Kampfgeistes viel Silber, damit sie in seiner Leibwache dienten. Das war die legendäre »Warägergarde«.

Wie die Wikinger lebten

Der Großteil der Wikinger lebte nicht vom Raub, sondern als friedliche Bauern, Fischer und Jäger. Sie wohnten auf weit verstreuten Höfen, die von dichten Wäldern umgeben waren. Es wurde Getreide angebaut und man hielt Rinder, Schweine und Schafe.
Im Winter gingen die Bauern im Wald auf die Jagd. Die Felle und das Gehörn der erjagten Tiere wurden in die Städte gebracht und verkauft. Dort konnte die Landbevölkerung im Gegenzug Schmuck und feine Stoffe, aber auch Sklaven erwerben.

In den Wikingerstädten lebten die Handwerker
und betrieben ihre Werkstätten.
Von den Kaufleuten bezogen sie die Rohstoffe
zur Herstellung ihrer Waren.
Die Händler bereisten mit ihren Schiffen die
gesamte damals bekannte Welt – von Grönland
bis in den fernen Orient.
Das allgemein gültige Zahlungsmittel in allen
Ländern der Wikingerzeit war Silber.

Die Behausungen

In den Häusern der Wikinger ging es beengt zu. Hier wurde gekocht, gegessen und geschlafen, aber auch gearbeitet. Im Inneren war es recht dunkel. Das Herdfeuer in der Mitte des Raums spendete ein wenig Licht und Wärme.
Der Rauch zog durch ein Loch im Dach ab.
An den Längsseiten befanden sich auf erhöhten Erdbänken die Schlafplätze. Einzig das Hausherrenpaar ruhte in einem richtigen Bett. Das war mit geschnitzten Tierköpfen verziert.
Sonst gab es nur wenige Möbel.

Die Hausherrin bestimmte über den Hof und das Gesinde, wenn der Mann auf Reisen war. Das Zeichen ihrer Stellung waren die Schlüssel an ihrer Kleidung, mit denen sie allein Zugang zu den Vorräten hatte.

1) Frau spinnt Wolle von einem Rocken auf eine Spindel.
2) offenes Herdfeuer
3) Truhe für die wertvollsten Gegenstände
4) Webstuhl, an dem man Tuch und Decke weben konnte
5) Lampe
6) Mahlstein, mit dem Getreide zu Mehl verarbeitet wurde
7) Bett des Hausherrenpaares

Sklave Freier Jarl

Gesetze und Bräuche

Die Bevölkerung der Wikinger bestand aus drei Schichten: den Leibeigenen, den Freien und den Häuptlingen.
Die Leibeigenen waren Sklaven und mussten für ihre Besitzer arbeiten. Oft waren sie auf den Raubzügen der Wikinger gefangen genommen worden und wurden dann verkauft.
Die Freien stellten den Kern der Gesellschaft. Sie waren meistens Bauern oder Handwerker.
Die Häuptlinge standen an der Spitze. Oft waren es mächtige und reiche Großbauern.
Die Vornehmsten nannte man »Jarle«. Aus dem Kreis der Jarle wurde der König gewählt.

Regelmäßig trafen sich die freien Männer zum »Thing«, um über wichtige Belange zu entscheiden, Gesetze zu erörtern oder Recht zu sprechen. Während dieser Zeit herrschte der Thingfrieden.
Viele Privatfehden wurden nicht vor dem Thing, sondern in einem Zweikampf ausgefochten. Dabei mussten die Widersacher auf einem ausgebreiteten Tuch gegeneinander antreten. Wer im Kampf unterlag, verlor seinen gesamten Besitz.
Deshalb wurden die Zweikämpfe oft bis zum Tode geführt. Der Gewinner galt als »von den Göttern beschützt«.

Die Götter der Wikinger

Vom christlichen Europa wurden die Wikinger als »Heiden« betrachtet, weil sie an eine Vielzahl von Göttern glaubten.
In der Vorstellung der Wikinger lebten die Götter an einem Ort namens Asgard und die Menschen in Midgard.
Die wichtigsten Gottheiten waren der Allvater Odin, seine Gattin Frigg, der jähzornige Donnergott Thor sowie die Liebes- und Fruchtbarkeitsgötter Freyja und Freyr.
Ihnen wurden Opfer dargebracht, um sie gnädig zu stimmen.

Die Wikinger glaubten auch an ein Leben nach dem Tod. Den Verstorbenen wurden Dinge des täglichen Gebrauchs, Waffen, Kleider und Schmuck mit ins Grab gelegt. Man nahm an, dass die Toten dies im Jenseits gut gebrauchen könnten. Könige und Fürsten wurden sogar mitsamt ihren Schiffen und Pferden beigesetzt.
Zur Erinnerung an Verwandte und Freunde errichteten die Wikinger Runensteine.
Das waren Gedenksteine mit Bildern oder Runen. Runen nennt man die Buchstaben der Wikingerschrift.

Wo sind die Wikinger geblieben?

Die Wikinger verursachten große Umwälzungen in Europa. Zunächst ängstigten sie ihre Zeitgenossen durch brutale Raubüberfälle und kriegerische Eroberungen. So werden die Wikinger auch heute noch oft beschrieben: als wilde, räuberische Kraftkerle auf Beutezug. Doch viel dauerhafter veränderte sich das Bild Europas durch die weltweiten Siedlungsfahrten und Handelsbeziehungen der Wikinger.
Sie pflegten ständigen Kontakt zu christlichen Ländern, wurden dort sesshaft und von Missionaren bekehrt.
Nach und nach schworen sie ihrem alten Glauben ab. Aus »Heiden« wurden Christen – und aus Wikingern wurden Dänen, Schweden und Norweger, Balten und Russen, Franzosen, Engländer, Deutsche, Iren oder Isländer!

Baffinland (Helluland)
Grönland
Labrador
(Markland)
Atlantischer
Ozean
Neufundland
(Vinland)
Heimatgebiet
der Wikinger
Handels- und
Eroberungszüge
von Wikingern
besiedelte Gebiete
Wikingernamen
1) L'Anse aux Meadow
2) (Brattahlid)
3) Westsiedlung
4) (Thingvellir)
5) Färöer
6) Shetland-Inseln
7) Dublin
8) Lindisfarne
9) York (Jorvik)
10) Bergen
11) (Kaupang)
12) Uppsala
13) (Birka)
14) Ribe
15) (Haithabu)
16) Hamburg
17) Aachen

Aralsee
Skandinavien
Reich der Rus
Kaspisches Meer
Schwarzes Meer
(Serkland)
Arabien
Mittelmeer
18) Rouen
19) Paris
20) Orléans
21) Sevilla
22) Konstantinopel (Miklagård)
23) Riga
24) Staraja Ladoga (Aldeigjuborg)
25) Nowgorod (Holmgård)
26) Kiew (Koenugård)
27) Bulgar
28) (Itil)
29) (Chorism)
30) Gorgan
31) Bagdad

Glossar

Frankenreich: Großes Reich im Westeuropa der Wikingerzeit, das sich vom heutigen Nordspanien, Frankreich, Österreich, Belgien, Holland bis nach Westdeutschland erstreckte.

Haithabu: Bekannter Handelsort der Wikinger, lag in der Nähe der heutigen Stadt Schleswig. Haithabu war mit etwa 1000 Bewohnern eine der größten Siedlungen im damaligen Nordeuropa!

Konstantinopel: Historischer Name der heutigen Stadt Istanbul. Zur Wikingerzeit Hauptstadt des Byzantinischen (Oströmischen) Reiches. Die Wikinger nannten sie »Miklagård«.

Normandie: Herzogtum an der Ärmelkanalküste des damaligen Frankenreiches, benannt nach den dort siedelnden »Normannen« (ein anderer Name für Wikinger).

Seidenstraße: Handelsweg, der den Orient mit den fernen Ländern Asiens verband.

DAS WILL ICH WISSEN

Hans Peter Thiel

Wale und Delfine

Katrin kennt sich aus mit Walen und Delfinen. Da kann sogar ihre Tante noch etwas von ihr lernen, denn die weiß nicht einmal, dass Wale keine Fische sind. Hier können Kinder das geheime Leben der faszinierenden Meeressäuger entdecken. Die bunten Illustrationen zeigen die großen und kleinen Walarten – denn es gibt Delfine, die nicht größer sind als ein Pinguin, und Blauwale so groß wie ein Flugzeug.

48 Seiten • Gebunden • Ab 6 Jahren • Mit zahlreichen farbigen Illustrationen

ISBN 978-3-401-06285-3

www.arena-verlag.de

Arena

DAS WILL ICH WISSEN

Burghard Bartos

Auf dem Ponyhof

Maries sehnlichster Wunsch geht in Erfüllung:
Für eine Woche darf sie auf dem Ponyhof Reiterferien machen. Dort lernt sie nicht nur reiten, sie erfährt auch viel über die Arbeit und das Leben auf einem Ponyhof. Und alle kleinen Pferdefans lernen mit ihr alles über Sattel und Zaumzeug, über Fütterung und Pferdepflege.

48 Seiten • Gebunden • Ab 6 Jahren • Mit zahlreichen farbigen Illustrationen

ISBN 978-3-401-06282-2

www.arena-verlag.de

Arena

DAS WILL ICH WISSEN

Margot Hellmiß

Die Feuerwehr

Tatütata, die Feuerwehr ...
Hier erfahren Kinder, was Feuerwehrleute alles machen – vom Feuerlöschen bis zum Einfangen entlaufener Zootiere. Die Leserinnen und Leser begleiten die Feuerwehrmänner bei spannenden Einsätzen und lernen auf anschauliche Weise die Aufgaben und die Ausrüstung der Feuerwehr kennen.

48 Seiten • Gebunden • Ab 6 Jahren • Mit zahlreichen farbigen Illustrationen

ISBN 978-3-401-06286-0

www.arena-verlag.de

Arena

DAS WILL ICH WISSEN

Rainer Crummenerl

Die Erde, unser Planet

Warum ist unsere Erde ein ganz besonderer Planet? Was befindet sich im Inneren der Erde? Wie sind die Meere und Kontinente, Berge und Flüsse entstanden? Und warum gibt es Erdbeben und Vulkane, Gewitter und Wirbelstürme? Mit vielen Erklärungen und aufschlussreichen Illustrationen zeigen diese Sachgeschichten ein spannendes Bild unseres blauen Planeten.

48 Seiten • Gebunden • Ab 6 Jahren • Mit zahlreichen farbigen Illustrationen

ISBN 978-3-401-06283-9

www.arena-verlag.de

Arena